ALL FOR TH

By the Same Author

Poetry

Picnic to the Moon 1944
Omens and Elegies 1951
Descent 1952
Three Elegies of Quintilius 1954
Images of Desire 1962
Elegy: Orpheus & Eurydice 1962
Dreamland and Drunkenness 1963
Complaints to Circe 1963
The Spirit and the Body 1963
Visions and Ruins 1964
Agamemnon in Hades 1965
The Golden Chain 1970
Paysages Légendaires 1972
The Elegies of Quintilius 1975
Ephemeron: An Epic Poem 1977
Theories 1978
Acts of Recognition 1979
Malice Aforethought 1982
Elemental Discourses 1982
Africa: A Dream 1982

Translations

Landscapes by Camillo Pennati 1964
The Concept of Comparative Philosophy by Henry Corbin 1981

Prose

An Examination of Ezra Pound [ed.] 1950, 1975
G.V. Desani 1952

Edited

NINE: A Review of Poetry and the Arts 1949–1956

PETER RUSSELL

All for the Wolves

Selected Poems 1947—1975

edited by Peter Jay

Anvil Press Poetry

Published in 1984
by Anvil Press Poetry Ltd
69 King George Street London SE10 8PX
ISBN 0 85646 095 8 cloth
ISBN 0 85646 096 6 paper

This book is published
with financial assistance from
the Arts Council of Great Britain

Printed and bound by Szeged Printing House, Hungary

for my wife, Lana Sue,
and our children, Kathleen, Sara, and Peter Parviz

Acknowledgement for permission to reprint certain poems in this book is made to the following publishers, reviews and editors: *Anglo-Welsh Review International Supplement* (ed. Vera Rich); *Antaeus* (ed. Daniel Halpern); the B.B.C. and Mr John Wain; Mr Richard Burns for a poem from *Homage to Mandelshtam*, Cambridge 1981; *Carleton Miscellany* (ed. Reed Whittemore); *City Lights Journal* (ed. Lawrence Ferlinghetti); Crescent Moon Press, Tehran, and Mr Peter Lamborn Wilson; *Delta* (ed. Louis Dudek); Hand and Flower Press and the late Erica Marx; Keepsake Press and Mr Roy Lewis; Mr Brian Keeble and the Golgonooza Press; *The Literary Review* (Fairleigh Dickinson University, N. J.); *Littack* and *The Littack Supplement* (ed. William Oxley); *Malahat Review* (ed. Robin Skelton); *New Measure* (ed. Peter Jay); *Poetry Quarterly* (ed. the late C. Wrey Gardiner); *The Southern Review* (ed. Donald E. Stanford); *Salzburg Studies in English Literature* (Dr Erwin A. Stürzl and Dr James Hogg), Institut für Anglistik, University of Salzburg. Apologies are made for any inadvertent omissions.

CONTENTS

Preface by PETER JAY 9

Poem for Peace 13
Ode ('Even as in summer...') 14
Ode ('Pine of Pontus...') 15
Snodgrass Who Died Last Week 16
Surya's Dance 17
Homage to Henri Rousseau 18
Nineteen Thirty-Seven 19
Ode to Evening 20
Melos 21
The Ruin 22
From The Elegies of Quintilius
    1 Daunia 24
    3 The Golden Age 26
Mandelshtam's Tristia 33
Khâqânî's The Ruins of Madâ'in 34
Memory 37
Evening in a Moroccan Café 38
'Asses en ont sofert la cuivre' 40
A Celebration 41
Berlin December 44
Mousai 46
Weihnachten 47
Three Songs 48
Winged Amor Painted Blind 50
Monday Morning 51
Claire de Lune 52
Elegiac 53
Missing a Bus 56
'Fallen Sie Langsam' 59
Delphi 60
Blind Homer 60
Boy Riding 61
Analogy 62
Leaving Germany 63
Dream Song 64

Verses Written in the Sand   65
In the Campo de la Bragora   66
The Golden Chain   67
Girl Painting   68
The River   69
For Ezra Pound's Eightieth Birthday   70
Night Resonance   71
Venice in Winter   72
Interim   73
The Dead Theatre   75
From a Hospital Window   77
Mnemosyne   78
Splitting the Century   79
Nineteen Twenty-Three   81
Moscow the Third Rome   82
Plum-Picking 1939   83
In a Suburban Garden   85
Charisma   87
Jajce   88
Tsara   89
Manuela's Poems   90
A Bone-Rattle   94
The Holy Virgin of Mileševa   96
In Memoriam. Osip Emilyevich Mandelshtam   100
Colophon   101
Smoke   102
Un país de pajaros   105
Four Snowmen and a Fifth   106
Theorem   109
The Act of Love   111
Brock   116
Elementary   119
Elegy at the Winter Solstice   120
The 'Progresse'   126

Notes   129

Index of Titles   151

PREFACE

The value of Peter Russell's contribution to English poetry may be known to fewer people today than when he was active as an editor and publisher during the fifties and early sixties. Since 1963 he has lived abroad, mainly in Venice, apart from some years in the mid-seventies which he spent in Canada, the USA and (until the Ayatollah Khomeini's revolution) Iran. His influence over many years as mentor, inspiration and guide to a number of younger poets and editors has been exemplary in its generosity and conviction. And yet his poetry has remained little known and appreciated. As befits one so distrustful of what he refers to as the 'mental *boutiques* and minimal art bazaars of the metropolis', he has been as careless of his standing with our reputation-makers as he has been committed to the art of poetry. As poet, scholar, critic, editor, translator and teacher, not to mention part-time bookseller and publisher, Peter Russell has professed poetry for forty years.

As a poet, he is prolific and protean. Since much of his work has until recently been semi-privately published, and much has only circulated among friends in manuscript, it seemed to me that a substantial retrospective selection would go some way towards providing a fairer picture of his work as a whole than has been available. As any selection from such an abundant oeuvre must be, the picture is only partial, and – though he has been unfailingly tolerant of my prejudices – the picture presented here is my description of his poetry, not Peter Russell's own.

I have tried to choose poems I like which, taken together, would illustrate the range and variety of his work over a period of nearly thirty years. I have drawn on the whole of his published verse, and from unpublished material kindly made available by Peter Russell and by Richard Burns. I have tried to keep a balance between short and longer poems, between lyrics and extended free-verse poems. Since his longer reflective poems have been recently collected and published as *Elemental Discourses* (University of Salzburg, 1982), I have chosen sparingly from them. Possibly the finest of his contemplative poems, *Paysages Légendaires* (Enitharmon Press, 1972), was not included in that collection; its length ruled out its inclusion here, and the poem proved resistant to my attempts to represent it by extracts.

I restrained myself with difficulty from including all six poems of *The Elegies of Quintilius,* long a favourite book of mine. The 1972 edition is still in print. Quintilius is for me the quintessential Russell persona, and I am glad to salute his re-emergence in the more recent poems 'Brock' and 'Elegy at the Winter Solstice'. To a general rule of no translations I have allowed two exceptions: the versions of Khâqânî's extraordinary 'The Ruins of Madâ'in', and (at Peter Russell's suggestion) Mandelshtam's 'Tristia', a poem which he regards as possibly the most influential poem, for him, of this century. (Peter Russell's versions of Mandelshtam printed in early issues of *Agenda* were among the first to introduce the great Russian poet's work into English.) I need hardly emphasise the degree to which Peter Russell's poetry is informed by his knowledge of the languages, literatures and philosophy of many cultures. He is a natural comparatist: his learning is extraordinarily wide-ranging, but it is not remotely academic, since the focus of his intellectual interests runs counter to the academic tendency towards ever narrower specialisation. 'Peter Russell has, all these years,' wrote Kathleen Raine, 'kept faith (as did his master Ezra Pound) with what is perhaps the greatest imaginative and philosophical conception of the European tradition, "the Beautiful". He is, like the Sufis, a poet of the drunkenness of the Spirit.'

The notes which Peter Russell has provided for this selection of his poems are more than just entertaining and informative. Behind the elaborate joke of his parodistic commentary on 'Elegy at the Winter Solstice', behind the façade of his satire on pedantry written in the same style as his notes to the 1972 edition of *The Elegies of Quintilius,* his concern for the values of the 'creative *mind*' and for the primacy of the Imagination emerges clearly. His view of poetry is unfashionable, traditional in the widest sense, and profoundly challenging.

This book was conceived in principle some ten years ago. It owes its appearance first to Peter Russell for his patient co-operation in the slow assembly of the selection, then to Richard Burns for his critical advice and encouragement: I thank them both for their generous help. I should also like to thank Caroline Root, Mrs Lana Russell and David McDuff for their valuable assistance in the book's preparation.

PETER JAY

All for the Wolves

POEM FOR PEACE

Black-headed gulls on the Thames

The hooded nuns hasten along the corridors,
Frantic the day's hours and the search for God.
Flags echo wars, and like the pain of peace
That cannot come this way, the gulls veer
Away over mountains of sea, dividing us.
Like nuns the gulls are hooded in my heart.

In winter the harsh cry of the wandering ones
Harries the earth's worms. Where is your hood
In winter, wandering gull, I wonder where?
Or when at summer's close you cast it off,
Gull, did you know that winter's war was near?
Hooded gull, my summer gull, put off your hood!

Chelsea, 1947

ODE

Even as in summer the thrush, even
As bones in the cavernous days
Or shells of spring, as the mothers' love,
As the young fauns' leaping fear,
Even as the road is long, even, uneven...

As the hart pants, as the fauns seek
Shade and the butterfly hesitates,
As the cuckoo mocks from the topmost twig
Where the sweet-apple hangs in the flower
And the apple-gatherers' coming is sure...

As the crushing of corn, of apples, of grapes,
The crushing of lips, the trampling
Of wishes and kisses underfoot like fruit
Where autumn waits with the Northern nymphs,
The burning of leaves and the season's agaric...

O Postumus, Kypria, we three have seen
The world's so frangible arrogance
And know its brief tears cannot prick
With pain or joy, or stab as a bird's song may
Or autumn's forming bones in the April egg.

Battersea, 1947

ODE

for Norman Callan

Pine of Pontus, aristocrat, what
Pride or lone-eagle arrogance
Is guarantee against the lover's
Tears, proof against the sun's
Hot ministry to the blood? Kings,
Priests, generals, unwitting peasants,
Free-thinkers and congratulators
Of themselves, have known the innocent sun's
Irresistible treachery. No name,
Established reputation or heraldic arms,
Greaves, breastplate, or steel vizard,
Can be protection against these naked
Boys, Sextus, who assail us in the streets
And threaten us with arrows and with rotten grapes.

London, 1948

SNODGRASS WHO DIED LAST WEEK

After he found the rags of flesh and the insistent
Hours of ennui; after the evening wanderings
Disconsolate through ruins with the blunted ends of pleasure;
After the memory rubbed like knuckles and knees
And the dusty leaves of an earlier life,
Middle-aged Snodgrass suddenly left the town.

He found home in an old shelter in the woods
With a dozen coloured panels on the walls depicting
An unimagined gaiety. Wet leaves
And the sound of rain refreshed him, and he lived
Content for nearly a year before he died.
Why should the corncrake disturb him in mild June
Or the raven in December?

London, 1948

SURYA'S DANCE

for Gloria Komai

Ram Gopal was the blood-red sun
Golden upon the leaves.
                      Above,
The green erotic bird arose
And the sword-bright rushes leapt
At the first gleam of his gilded ancient coronal.

The tawny panther smouldered in the glade,
The ephemeridae danced madly in the air.

London, 1948

HOMAGE TO HENRI ROUSSEAU

Cobras like arms charmed by the dark
Flautist, vertical swords passive
By the muddy river, the hirsute begonia-
Like leaves a shade for the strange
Musician of the Jungle – I am afraid
In the moving gloom of snakes and
Hidden birds; afraid to gaze
Up at the pallid huntress, who
Lie mesmerised and trembling in
The sodden darkness at her feet.
Bright flame-tips of rushes and bent
Girders of vapid greenery, I
Am doomed to be victim here to a
Charmer of snakes and waiting flamingoes,
Who wait in the inky twilight of dreams.

London, 1948

NINETEEN THIRTY-SEVEN

Brean Down, Somerset

What were the longshore, the weathers, the peculiar flutings,
And the marram-dunes distant from us there
Ankle-deep among worn-out cockle-shells on the shore?
What were the rock-pipit, the curlew or the gulls,
Mockers of marsh and shoreland, the buried cowrie,
Leopard-painted and precious to a child's unrewarded eye?
What were the foam and scud of the weary sea at night
Or the silence of deserted dunes icy from
Lack of sun?   A child buried his eager
Hands in the midnight sand and lay for an hour
Listening to the sleeping earth and the restless sea,
And the occasional cries of waking unseen birds.
What were the shooting-stars, the summer-lightnings,
The gun-flashes portending war, and
The lighthouse-beam all-night-revolving,
The spoke of a wheel? The long-eared owl, the nightjar,
Spoke at descending evening of inevitable night,
Silent and black, or lit by the pellucid moon,
To a scarecrow child frightened by the shore.
At dawn the assembling marsh-birds in innumerable choir,
Hidden in gun-metal air or the first gleams
Of light reflected from water lying like lead,
Heavy on sand, and the land-birds too, small
Pencils of sound from stunted trees on the dunes,
Woke to the day: day that was ordinary and difficult
To understand though the night's darkness was full of
        prophesies.
What were the hidden bugles, the sun-spots, and the sounds
Of the armies of heaven and hell marching on our heads,
The voices in clouds, and the stupendous comet that never
Came, and the eternally ominous rumbling of the sea?

London, 1948

ODE TO EVENING

O bright particular star, Heaven-shiner,
    Each evening folding by thy influence
    Into darkness and despair, O where
        Goes Ceres now?

In the remote green dingles with unsandalled feet
    In mists or at the edge of woods
    Reapers have seen her pass, her head
        In sorrow bowed,

Her white hands welcoming descending night,
    Oblivion's poppies sending as a gift
    Like kisses lost to also wandering
        Orpheus.

Dismiss those humble bureaucrats thy bees
    Into their flowery granaries of woe,
    Wither these strange bright flowers of day
        Into shut ease,

Bestow thy ancient bounty on the world,
    Nocturnal euthanasia for all that go
    Searching for lost meanings and desires of old
        On Gaia's paths.

Bright lantern lead sad travellers on!
    Dimming dear hopes with thy wise prose
    Provide new light as purple turns
        To indigo.

Let thy blue shadows hide the idle scythe
    In corners, while the late-kindled fire
    Responds to thine; provide sweet fruits
        For tables set.

O star, persist until oncoming night
    Take finally direction from thy beam;
    And bid her hide each anxious fugitive
        From his own gloom.

London, 1949

MELOS

for T. W. Ramsey

So big the island! Who would know what calm
Engenders in the bones of men their rest?
Less than a requiem but far more blest
Than sleep beneath the shadow of a palm,
This island happiness is like a psalm
Melodious, triumphant to the breast,
Yet larger, sweeter, never fearing lest
Some god or man should take away its balm.

Each landsman knows all island beauty is
Environed by the sea, untouched by snow,
Its sons unherded like the mainland sheep
Or stars unnoticed in the galaxies.
This calm is of a single star, its glow
Is afternoon unending, summer's sleep.

London, 1949

THE RUIN

I

Bullfinch pilfers the apple-bud
Chaffinch scours the ground
Men in the woods remember
Philomel's wound
Raking the magic ember

Shrewmouse nests
By the compost-mound
Magpie omnivorous thief
Sinister black and white
Ravages waste for his food
And the red kite

The fat grey goose
Seizes the bud and the leaf

II

The greenfinch in the hedge
The warbler in the sedge
Day long
Give forth their song
At the Town's edge
Flame shall lick the wood of the door
Timbers crash and crush the floor

Every green thing
Invades the town
Roots will lever
Great stones down
Creeper cover
The gonfaloun

The raven sit on the fallen porch
Owl be the City's only torch
Nightjar thrum

Where was oppidum
Jackdaw sleep
In the ruined keep

No maid shall weep   No maid shall weep

III

Bullfinch pilfers the apple-bud
Chaffinch scours the ground
There are men in the woods
There are men in the woods

And the wild geese go with their gaggling sound

Sussex, 1951

from The Elegies of Quintilius

1: DAUNIA

Generous wick with the oil of the coconut palm
Kindling each evening our own nuptial flame,
Witness you were of the love-act a number of times
Nightly, in the city of Sfax in my youthful days,
Till Daunia left me to shiver in an empty bed.
She it was who originally insisted on this
Petting and kissing by lamplight till long after dawn
Made weak the once-upright flame at our bedside.
Possible outcomes or permanency never entered
Our heads that were full of sex-games and gladiators;
The arena by day and the dust of our bed by night
With the trim wick glowing, and the wail of musicians
On the other side of the forum, with flutes and a drum
Loading the evening air with voices and wine,
Kept us too busy for thoughts of a home or of infants.
Now she has left me, now she's run off with another
(Rotten scum of a fellow from Rome with more
Gold in his purse than ever my father had
Before the drachma crashed and the markets went dead), –
With him she's gone off, they leave on the next boat for Rome.
She knocked on my door in the morning to say goodbye
'Don't weep, Quintilius, you will soon find another nice girl
To warm you in bed and wash your hair before sleep.
You'll forget your sweet Daunia long before she
Ceases to long for a former lover in Sfax.'
I couldn't bear to hear more of these words, so quickly
Went out into the backyard with the chickens
And wept, leaving the rest of her message to fall
On the polished brass knocker, my father's pride.
I had often thought I was going to end up a failure;
At the worst I had thought 'This girl will be a good
Wife to me now I'm a failure at everything else
Unbraiding her hair in the evening and lulling our babes
To sleep as the sun goes down on our modest house',

But had never troubled to ask her. Now she has gone,
And the bright streets of Rome will claim her the rest
Of her girlish days. Perhaps I shall die single
Not troubling to cook myself breakfast or
Keep more than a few half-bottles in the house
Of cheap red wine, and a jar of black olives.
Delicacies cost such a lot –
Without her to want an occasional bracelet
I shall die with my palms clean of the dust of gold
And be none the worse off. 'O Mother Venus
What can your poor sons do deserted by girls
They have ever taken for granted? It hurts.
Send either another Greek courtesan
Who is tired of life in the brothels, and is seeking a home
Modest enough for dull me to provide for,
Or end this unnecessary slowness of days.
I'll make her a good husband I promise you;
Just find me a house with a field not too far from the city
With space enough for chickens, a cock, a pig and a cow:
Let it have three or four gnarled and split olive-trees
With ripe berries in early November; let it
Have ample room for the winter-wheat and a terrace
Of large-leaved vines for the summer months.
And don't forget to remind your old father
To make sure there's rain when it's needed. Dear Goddess
I'd soon take root at the edge of the city of Sfax
Provided my new wife doesn't turn out a scold
And further invasions don't interrupt the quick-footed hours
With parties of homeless and hungry looking for food.'
What a fool I was not to ask that girl at the time:
Her soft fingers made sweet our evening food
And she never refused to delight in the joys of Love.
I doubt I shall find another, at least in this age.

London, 1949

As long as the unripe figs keep dropping outside our door
So long will my modest hopes keep falling away.
A time there was when I envisaged a future
Of peace in the country, tillage of fruitful vines,
Lifelong possessions including a house with a terrace,
Clean water-pipes and plenty of nearby firewood
To keep at bay the frosty invasions of winter;
A few books on a dry shelf, the visits of friends
From far-off countries (occasion for slaying a calf
And serving the tired travellers with rich Falernian
And the good beast's tasty brains in black butter);
Nightlong discussion of poets, the meaning of ancient myths,
– The seeding-time, it might be, of our own hoped-for masterpieces
To ensue at the end of our banquets, – happiness thus, I believed.
But sitting here disgruntled, with a poor copyist's text
(Garbled, misspelt and full of interpolations,
Sadly misinterpreted by the ass-eared Doctors of Rome),
What should I do but weep, hearing as the hours go by
Fig after fig crash down through the cool green leaves
To splash on the gloomy earth, a prey to ravenous insects.
O, dear bountiful Mother, what fool was it, I ask
Who planted thy fig-tree in unfriendly shadows
So that only the topmost fruits received the boon of the Sun
Ripening in warm purple wrinkles to feed thy ministrant?
Nor was it suitably cared for, this overgrown arbor,
So that not reaching the highest boughs I am left
With nothing but hard pellets of unripe figgery.
Many things stand in doubt: – Of this alone are we certain –
All worthy things demand an expense of labour: all
Potentially fertile tracts must be driven with many canals,
And branches too-speedily sprouting need to be skilfully pruned
Through toilsome hours of sweat-bringing sun;
Just, O Apollo, as thy melancholy youths must fit
Their sad singing into ordered shapes of woe,
Or, Priapus, thy merry worshippers their shouts.
Mutandae sedes: I cannot abide this condition;
Moderate recognition, reasonable availability of books

And some slight hope of enduring Peace might have stayed
Me from my unhappy wandering over the face of Europe,
Asia and Africa, seeking through men and books
The good life. Iniquity, it seems, has as many faces
As now there are wars on earth: even for poets this life
Is one without honour, integrity – without even shame.
Where once sang ancient bards, base slaves are rising to cushy jobs
Well-paid in the Civil Service, Universities, cultural bodies,
And other, as it were, metropolitan latifundia.
All values are reversed where cowardice is a virtue
And courage by many considered a shameful affectation,
Where to speak but of 'heroes' or indite the deeds of the noble
Assuredly marks out a fool, prevents all preferment
And makes him more enemies than there are bum-boys in Sybaris.
Before all things however, it is meet to revere the Gods:
This I have always believed, and I hope that I always shall.
Yet now they are saying it is no good to invoke the old gods –
Weak men have overthrown Almighty Jupiter the King,
Juno, men say, they have put to shame, Heaven's Queen.
I do not know what to say but of this I am certain –
Beneficent spirits, as well as malignant, exist.
This new god who unites all our slaves against us,
Cutting from under our feet the best in the ancient order,
Overladen with ethics and poisoned with ugly politics,
Has weakened the rule of the good, replacing the Ancient Justice
With courts full of slaves, Orientals and Vandals
Each taking his none too small commission
On the fruits of individual freedom. It stinks,
This centralisation of every separate faculty,
This systematic attrition of the old individual ethics.
Responsibility is robbed from the private citizen
And sold back soiled to the public at higher prices
By the insufferable rabble of once Imperial Rome,
Constantinople, Ravenna and Naples. Ye Gods, what a crew
Of filth and corruption fills now the seats of our ancient councils!
To Venus, I pray, Apollo, Minerva and Mars
To throw out this coprophilious mob and burn their remains,
Leaving unburied and nameless their oleaginous ashes.
For me, I must ply the vowed toils of the dedicated poet,
Lay-priest to Apollo, servant of virtuous people,

Scholar and devotee of every Art and Science,
And at all times attendant to the visiting Muse,
– Knocked senseless and left hungry as I may be
By hostile Fates and the murderous hands of men.
Here I must stay, composing my stubborn verses
Until I have sold enough produce here in the markets of Cagnes
Again to weigh anchor and move to more friendly parts.
Me indeed, above all, may the sweet Muses welcome with gifts,
(Whose sacred emblems driven by absorbing love I bear);
To me, their servant, may they show the ways of Heaven and
    the stars,
Sun's daily setting, and the Moon's diverse phases;
The cause of earthquakes; and the force that makes Ocean heave
Breaking its barriers now, now sinking in its allotted basin;
Why it is that Winter's suns hasten so to dip themselves
Beneath the sea; and what delay detains the tardy nights.
Thy countryside and all Thy running streams
Be my delight, sweet Goddesses; and let me love
Thy waters and secluded woods. There no resounding cries
Of injured fame shall call, or interrupt the Hours.
Let me come forth at times, a fugitive, from woods,
Alone to mingle in the crowds, unknown at Erraginum,
Or attend, unseen, the rites of Mithra at Nemausis.
And may I meet peace-loving tribes by the way
Dancing their secret rituals in hidden groves
Where Bacchus and the nymphs are frequent visitors
Bringing sweet wine and generous love. And may I know
Cool glens, and dwell in the shade of huge branches.
Happy is he who has learned of the causes of things,
Overcome every intruding fear and laid at his feet
Unyielding Fate and awful-voiced Acheron the greedy.
Happy also is he who has known the countryside gods –
Pan, Silvanus and all the nymphs their lovely sisters.
Him neither popular honours nor the purple of kings,
Nor Discord stirring up brother and brother, can bend;
Nor the united strength of outer barbarian tribes,
Established might or any power about to fall: nor shall he grieve
With pity for the oppressed or envy of the rich.
The fruit that this man picks his willing fields
And branches of their own choice bear; he does not know

The ridiculous Forum or the stubborn Laws,
Or even the Tabularium with its lists of all the people
Meticulously copied out like the pedigrees of goats:
His wisdom is small but great is the folly of rulers.
There have been times, and gladly I confess this truth,
When I have dreamed, pent up in the Ligurian hills –
(Where once Boëbius the Praetor on his way to Spain
Died of his wounds before the Roman sway
Tamed the fierce hill-men or decreed this everlasting Province;
Boëbius Pamphilus, Fabius Buteo and other worthy Romans
Failed to subdue this race: but when Republican ambassadors
Landed from ships upon the pebbled shore and offered terms,
And, shamefully put to flight, bent anxious sails to Mother Rome
Swearing revenge, Quintus Opimius, consul, with his fleet
Carrying the 22nd legion, reached scorched Oegitna's beach.
Oegitna falls, bloody repressions follow, and a harsh campaign;
Antipolis is taken, the Oxybians fall back in rout,
Their prisoners enslaved, their leaders sent in chains to Rome;
Onepia suffers a like fate after a bloody battle in the plain
When the heroic Deciati lend aid to Oxybian remnants:
Both tribes being subjugated and a final treaty composed.
In such a manner was the Roman rule
Extended from Cisalpine Gaul to once-Greek Massilia,
And through Narbonne to Spain. Eighty long years it took
As Strabo says, to win a narrow strip of land along
Ligurian shores from Italy to the Iberian border
For the sake of 'public services') – but I digress:
Times there have been when in Ligurian hills
Quintilius dreamed a space and all was changed –
The learned Muses on their sacred mountains praised
And Arts and Sciences pursued for Virtue's cause
(Not the foundations of rich merchants or the schools
Open to all and propped up hypocritically with funds
Extorted from the purse of each unthinking citizen):
Here in the little oppidum of Cagnes all trace of human crime
Shall disappear; a leader shall arise
To teach each Province of the weary world its way
To a new age when wars shall cease and harsh times grow gentle;
Under his tutelage the rising States of Barbary shall calm
Their bloody longing to subdue the entire world,

And, schooled to the ancient rule of pastoral life,
They and the elders of each country that has known
Ravages of war, of slavery the sharp distress,
Remembrance of great happiness in time of woe,
Assembling all the wise and virtuous of their towns
Shall formulate the pattern of the age to come.
Money shall be abandoned, purveyors of false wealth
Expelled from the confines of this fortunate Empire;
Arms, and the whole cumbrous industry of war,
Deemed useless, shall give way to cultivation of rich crops.
Corn, vines and vegetables in profusion shall be tilled,
The hornet shall bring forth honey in hives like the bee,
The scorpion go stingless and the snake with blunted fang,
The wild beasts turn tame and ally themselves with men
Sharing both food, and labour the bringer of food,
Lying down by the ass and the kid, no longer a menace
To grass-eating herds or peaceful men.
Apollo shall restore daily Sun to the earth yet never scorch
The tender seedlings or ever parch the throat of the rough goat.
Friendly fire will crackle on the hearth, licking damp logs,
Yet in summer the mountain forests shall be safe from burning.
Each night the sweet earth warmed by the daytime sun
Shall drink its fill, but no more, of fragrant rainwater.
Hot Afer and sudden Notus shall no longer bend the crops
Or hurl to destruction sea-going fishermen;
A light breeze will play over the housetops
Sparing the midday sleeper from stagnant heats:
Nature herself unite joyfully all her forces
Henceforth to give glad seasons to a peaceful race of men.
Remote tribes shall be pacified: their mountain streams
Run wines of every kind – Methymnian pour by the side
Of Rhaetic, Mareotic and Psithian; tenuous wines of Lagea
Cut the feet from under the fiercest bibbers;
Yet shall the fair fumes of every brew but clear the head
Bringing at last to the willing pilgrims of Bacchus
Exquisite visions, conversation unequalled for all
That the worthy ancients ever considered virtuous;
Aminean wines and the long-lasting lesser Argitis
Stand ready at every board; at Bacchus' behest
Poets shall rise to recite, reviewing the feats of Troy

And the unconquered Greeks, telling of Dardan Aeneas
And the tears of Dido; making new epics of Marius
The Deliverer, of murdered Cicero and the Divine Augustus:
Odes, elegies and Tyrian idylls will pass the hours
In dulcet singing to the lyre and fife, Lyaeus King:
Nay more, the wine-God brings wines that shall vie in sweetness
With hitherto unrivalled Falernian vintage;
Distant Lusitania and unknown isles of the Western Sea
Shall bring forth honey-scented heavy delicious liquors
Challenging sweetness known only before in Sicily;
From Aquitania a new imperial wine, fruiting profusely,
Shall supply the tables of princes through the world; to the North –
Castrum Divionense be witness – wonderful grapes shall grow,
Giving honour to Gaul and a new nectar to all men.
Yet neither Media's groves (that rich terrain),
Nor lovely Ganga, Hermus thick with gold,
Fragrant Panchaea, Bactra nor the East
Vie in repute with easeful Italy;
She is the home of olives and of joyous herds,
Hers is eternal Spring; Summer in every season;
Twice fruit the trees and twice in calf are the heifers heavy;
Neither the lion nor the cruel tiger is hers
Nor does the poison aconite deceive the unwary,
Nor the great coiled serpent threaten a dreadful death.
Silver, copper and gold run in the streams
Of this country – Saturnian Tellus! Great Parent of fruits
And of men, to Thee I dedicate my song
Of ancient art and many-chanted praise.
Yet – two thousand years hence they will still hunt the wolf
In the beautiful Alban hills and peace be still a stranger to men.
Mankind was never made equal: degree is the will of the Gods;
Every attempt to change it ends with disaster.
Innocent hope is the laughing-stock of the wise.
Alas though, it flounders in Night, as though it were plunged
    in Orcus,
This Godless race we belong to. Each in his own endeavour
Weaves his destruction. Madly the savages labour
Unresting, but fruitless their work as the Furies'.
And so it will be, till wakened from fitful sleep
Young once again and pure, Man goes in the fields

As often he did in the blossoming gardens of Hellas,
A new age breathed by the Spirit of Nature,
Paths of the verdant Earth made known to all men.
Ye Gods, what boots it to imagine or to hope!
Alas, it was a dream; Quintilius sits alone,
Sipping that Lotus-brew which the Gauls of this region
Distil from the benevolent husks of well-dried poppy seeds.
The dull fig falls flat on the ground in the noonday heat,
The gadfly lurks in the empty meadow.

Cagnes-sur-Mer, 1950

TRISTIA

from the Russian of Osip Mandelshtam (1918)

I have learned the whole art of leave-taking
In bare-headed night-lamentations.
The oxen chew: anticipation lingers –
It is the last hour of vigils in the city;
And I honour the ceremony of that cock-crying night
When raising their burden of sorrow for a departing traveller
Eyes that were red with weeping gazed into the distance
And the wailing of women mingled with the song of the muses.

In that word 'leave-taking' who can tell
What kind of separation is in store for us,
What it is the crying of cocks promises
When fire burns on the acropolis:
And in the first red dawn of some new life
When lazily the ox is chewing in the shade,
Why does the cock, the new life's own town-crier
On the city wall beat madly with his wings?

I love the way the thread is spun –
The shuttle runs to and fro, the spindle hums –
Look now – already like swansdown
Barefooted Delia flies to meet you!
O the meagre pattern of our life –
Even our happiest words are threadbare!
Everything has been of old and will be again:
For us, only the moment of recognition is sweet.

So let it be: the little gleaming figure
Lies on the spotless earthen dish.
Like the stretched-out skin of a squirrel,
Stooping over the wax the young girl gazes.
It is not for us to guess about Grecian Erebus:
What's bronze for man for woman is only wax.
Our destiny befalls us only in battles –
They see the future as they die.

translated Sussex, 1958

THE RUINS OF MADÂ'IN
a qasîda of Khâqânî

Now O heart that has seen Time's lessons, – look now with your
  eyes!
Know now! Madâ'in's courts are a mirror of lessons!
Make your way to the Tigris! Make your dwelling in Madâ'in!
From your eyes make a second Tigris flow!
Tigris itself weeps so, – you will say 'It is a hundred rivers of blood!'
From the heat of its lifeblood fire is licking its lashes.
You see the Tigris's lips, – how froth forms at its mouth,
As though its lips were blistered by the heat of its sighs.
See now Tigris's heart roasted in sorrow's fire!
Did you ever hear of water that's scorched by fire?
Weep again and again upon Tigris! With your eyes give a tithe! –
Though the shore of the sea receives its own tithe from Tigris.
If Tigris set its lips' sighs to the fire of its burning heart,
Half will be turned to sad embers, half to a blaze of fire.
Till the Chain of the Palace in Madâ'in was broken in Madâ'in
Tigris itself was in chains, for it writhed like a chain.
From time to time cry out then on the Palace in the language
  of tears
Till you hear in the ear of your heart the Palace's answer!
The toothed walls of each echoing court give you answer again
  and again!
Hear the advice of the topmost teeth
From the earth at the walls' feet, that were toothed!
It says: 'You are made of dust, – we are your dust now!'
Take two or three steps upon us, shed a tear or two also!
From the wailing cries of the owls we have all got headaches!
With the tears of your eyes make mudpacks and cure our headaches!
It is no wonder that in the world's green meadow
The owl comes after the bulbul, wailing after sweet song.
We are the Palace of Justice! This persecution overcame us!
What calamity will come to the Palace of the persecutors
  themselves?
It is as though the Palace that was towered like the firmament
  was overturned! –

Was it the behest of the turning World or of Him who turns
    the World?
You laugh at what my eyes are weeping for here.
It is those who do not weep here at the last shall be laughed at.
The old woman of Madâ'in is not less than Kufeh's old woman!
The narrow cell of the one is not less than the other's oven!
Make of your breast an oven! Of your eye demand a storm!
This is that same Palace the dust before whose Gates
Was a picture gallery's wall from the print of men's faces.
This is that same Entrance Gate where once waited kings!
Its guard was the Emperor of Babylon, Turkestan's King was
    its slave!
This is that same Throne from whose majestic awe
Lion-bodied Shadravan assaulted the Lion of the World!
Imagine! – This is that same Time, – see with the Eye of
    Contemplation!
In the Chain of the Gateway, in the pomp of the Court
Dismount from your horse, bow your face on the chessboard
    of earth!
(Pawn taken by knight, castle levelled to the ground!)
Beneath his Elephant's foot, see Na'man the Vazir, a king defeated!
(Queen taken by Bishop, the King in check!)
Alas! like Na'man, see the elephant-slayers of Kings!
The Day's and the Night's elephants have slain him with Time's
    trampling!
How many elephant-slaying Kings have been overthrown by the
    elephants' Kings,
The chessboard of their destiny become the mating-place of
    privation?
The Earth is drunk because it has drunk instead of Wine
In the bowl of Hormuz's skull the blood of Anushiravan's heart, –
For as many counsels as were manifested in the living crown of
    his head
A hundred new counsels now are hidden in his head's dead
    marrow.
Kasreh and his Golden Orange, – Parviz and his Quince of Gold, –
Are altogether gone with the wind, are utterly levelled with
    the dust!

Parviz at each banquet spread out his Apron of Gold on the
    ground;
He made from his stock of gold a gold-laden cloth like a garden of
    scents!
Parviz is now lost to this world! Speak less of Him who is lost!
Where is the Gold Cloth spread for that feast? Go put on the
    cloth of Contrition!
Where are these Standards, you ask, – where are those crowned
    heads now?
The womb of the Earth is pregnant with them for ever!
So late, with such pains, the pregnant Earth brings forth!
It is easy to sow the seed – to give birth is difficult!
The Wine that the vine's root gives is the blood of the heart of
    Shirin!
The vat that the peasant sets forth is made from Parviz's water
    and clay!
So many bodies of tyrants are swallowed up in this dust, –
This greedy-eyed earth even now is not satiated with them!
From the blood of the hearts of children it mixes rouge for its face!
This old man with the white eyebrows, this old woman with black
    breasts!
Khâqânî, – beg for advice from this door
Till at your door himself the Emperor begs!
If an artful beggar craves sustenance from the Sultan today
Tomorrow the Sultan may ask sustenance from the beggar's door!
If the Road to Mecca is a 'gift to every City'
Take then a gift from Madâ'in, sustenance from the foot of
    Shirvan!
Everyone takes from Mecca a rosary of the earth of Hamzeh;
So you too, – from Madâ'in take a rosary of the earth of Salman!
Look on this Sea of Insight! Do not pass by without drinking,
For from such a Sea's gulph the lips can never get thirsty.
Brothers who come from the Road bring a present:
This poem is a present for the Heart of Brothers!
See what a Mystery is driven forth in this poem! –
A corpse with a heart like Christ!
A mad fool with a Wise Soul!

translated London, 1961

MEMORY

I count the grains of sand on the beach and measure the sea;
I understand the speech of the dumb and hear the voiceless.
There is room for everything in the neutral process of time.
I touch the taste of the past and feel the future –
It is no good aiming at beauty – you will miss the mark.
Match words with ideas, sensations with sentences.
Beauty is the supervening perfection, *epigignomenon ti telos*
Inherent in the finished work, unimagined at the start
And certainly not intended. Pleasure cannot be known –
It is there in the dark with Psyche, the gift of a God.
You work with complete absorption unabashed as a lover –
Pleasure is with you till you try to look at her face,
Then is gone. And the beach is deserted and the mouth voiceless
That utterly enchanted you that summer.

Kent, 1962

EVENING IN A MOROCCAN CAFÉ

Evening and the homing bees – that tune! – a bright
Particular star that will be shining soon,
A plate of cus-cus and an Arab girl
With bloodless lips the colour of a mole.
Never a word exchanged to note our thinking,
Only a heady lull drenched with Moroccan wine.

The sunset bled across the sky like rough red wine
Staining its azure linen that had been so bright
(It came invisibly at first and far too soon),
It softened gently with its glow an Arab girl's
Grey lips that moved as silent as a mole,
Spitting the grape-pips out as she sat thinking.

All evening in the rose and grey we sat there thinking,
Drinking the cooling air like a light wine.
'That tune' came back, that star became more bright
And more particular and large, more soon
Than any words could come to that dark girl
Who gazed across the harbour to the mole.

A warship lay at anchor near the mole.
Perhaps it was of it that she was thinking
When finally she moved to pour the wine.
Her lips parted and her teeth showed small and bright
For just a moment, but they closed too soon
To catch the accent of that Arab girl.

To catch the accents of an Arab girl
Above the dialect of bees or squeak of mole
You have to sense, at first, what she is thinking.
You frown, and light a cigarette, and pour more wine
And notice how the flame of spirit shows up bright
In the first twilight that will be darkness soon.

You hope that she will break the silence soon
And tell the secrets of a silent girl.
Low on her throat you see another mole
Black on magnolia. And you are thinking
How cool her neck looks, her mouth that's full of wine
How full of kisses, and her eye how bright.

You did not notice that her eye was bright
Till suddenly she spoke, and 'I'll be going soon'
Squeaked in the high-pitched French of a schoolgirl.
And with a ringless pale-brown finger touched the mole
And sighed and simply said 'I have been thinking.'
You smiled. She went. You poured yourself more wine.

'That tune!' – a girl with moles, but she was gone too soon.

London, 1963

'ASSES EN ONT SOFERT LA CUIVRE'

(Jean Bodel, Le Feu de Saint Nicolas, c. 1190)

      ... is the deep urge
The descent into Avernus

Likewise the flaming road to the sun
The setting forth on seas
And disappearance into forests

      ... is universal like a god
A sacrifice that is offered
At the right season

Only the brave shall see
      the holy flowers of Paradise

The green grass of battle tinted red with blood

Murglies the Treacherous, Durindal, Joyeuse
Hauteclere and Precieuse of Babylon
Have fought their battles and been laid aside

The Hero sleeps beside the Bride

So wearily he winds his horn
      it's like a dying man

Under a pine-tree by a wild rose

London, 1963

A CELEBRATION

Life is a celebration not a search for success.
In the grey street to see visions of violet roses
And snow-buntings crowding in the black grass of the gutter;
A solitary heron with an eel in its beak
Circling the Stock Exchange. It is life, not death,
Celebration, not success, we must offer
To our wives, our children, our mistresses...

The unshaven merchant refuses you credit and shrugs –
You spit in the shining gutter and laugh in the wings of the sun.
You need not an obol to savour the perfume of roses,
To lie on the hot sands of the dunes naked with the goddess
Gently plucking the marram-tuft of her body
Roseate in the sun.
                    At dawn they take down the shutters –
At sunset they put them up. They carry the cash to the bank
Making increase of children by night as a habit.

The rock-pipit spies on our love-play, the curlew
Pierces the slow stichomythia of love in the afternoon
While the tills ring out unheard in the city and the suburban trains
Pointlessly run to and fro. The money-god laughs
Between the leaves of account-books – Aphrodite is bored
And sleek white swans whirr in the tepid air of the sunset.

All this you can see for yourself, dispossessed one!
Do you remember the Divine King – how he put down his golden
    crown
On the bare-earth floor of his reed-thatched palace
And went out in the fields with the shepherds and oxherds –
How stripped to the waist, his sacred loincloth twined above his
    knees,
He cut new reeds by the river and bound them,
Lifting great bundles on to the backs of us stooping peasants...
Slowly followed us back to the village?
He was the best thatcher there – the Goddess smiled on him.
That was a long summer then...

Barbarians came bringing copper and tin;
Stone celts lay on the ground unused,
Brambles grew over them. It was easier to work the new metals
For those who knew of a forge – you may laugh at the heaps of
    old iron
Reddening by disused railway-tracks –
Do not forget the bronze spear of savage Achilles
Or the winged speech of his golden mouth
Supreme among noble words, admonishing Priam
'Wretched things are we men, and the Gods,
Themselves without cares, have woven
Sorrow into the very pattern of our lives.'
                          Do not forget
Eleven days respite he gave to the hard-pressed Trojans...
Remember him pacing the white sands down by the ships,
How he fell on his face and wept for his slaughtered friend,
Clutching the sharp grains in his hands and gnashing his teeth –
At night he slept by the lovely Briseis
But never touched her...

Troy was sacked and destroyed but not until after
A sniper picked off god-like Achilles with a poor shot
That all but missed his heel. Destiny is what happens,
Whether it is written before or after the event,
And there is no escaping it – 'For of all creatures
That breathe and creep about the earth
There is none more wretched than man.'

Brush the sand from your mouth, earthly lover;
Stretch your naked limbs in the cool weightless waters
Of the evening air, when the burning sand grows cool to the touch,
And the violet sea turns dull like mud...
The heroic moment of love cannot last for ever –
Like a cloud from the sea it is distilled
By the slow watch in the office from long mahogany hours...

It is the high price of human purposiveness
That we do not sing all day like cicadas,
That the short hours of life are not all everlasting instants
Of unthinking praise like a single note

Of the nightingale's song, or the croaking of frogs.
We never repeat ourselves, every word that we utter
Is unique in its context, and instinct is only
The bare skeleton of our personalities.

Go to the graveyard, raise up the dead!
Listen to their rattling gait as they hobble about,
Fleshless and breathless twittering like distant sparrows.
Can you tell one from another
As their lower jaws soundlessly flap up and down
And the loose teeth rattle in the sockets?
This one had long hair, close rounded breasts
And a tongue like honey, and that
A voice like the thrush's song in March...

Our flesh nourishes the earth leaving only
Books – paper and ink of history – carious residue.

Without celebration, there is only a flapping of jaws,
Banging of doors in the wind

Where once Troy was

Double-entry accounts all correct
On papyrus of reed-thatch
Wood pulp
Megalopolis...

London, 1962

BERLIN DECEMBER

for Lydia Pasternak

The air is very cold and still,
    The factory-roofs remotely gleam;
The frost has etched the window-sill
    With leaves and twigs as in a dream.

The atmosphere is saturated
    With snow that's waiting in the sky –
Its white will be precipitated
    And drop down lightly from on high –

For now the air is like a pond
    No wind disturbs or fish excites,
And the soft silence spreads beyond
    The railway-tracks and concrete lights.

Like a stone hulk on ocean's floor
    Where all's been still for centuries,
There is no motion any more
    In what were once tremendous seas.

And what were once tremendous seas
    Seem calm now like a day of prayer,
After great slaughter or disease
    When men are contrite everywhere.

These icy doldrums! Still no peace
    Or more than breathing-space or pause!
For Nature, shaping histories
    Is always sharpening her claws –

Her claws that scratch at mountain-tops
    And scrape with fury ocean's floors,
That batter down the standing crops
    And beat upon the soul's weak doors.

This winter morning like a dream
    That has subtracted time from space,
Has changed my words to clouds of steam
    And turned the grimy twigs to lace –

The frost no longer seems to bite,
    The air is like a woollen shawl –
A soundless noise of flaking light
    Like diatoms, – snow starts to fall.

Berlin, 1963

The white body of my Beloved
Is a stone on which is inscribed
All dithyrambs psalms and epics
Shaped of the winged and holy words
Whether of holy Sion or of Helicon
Inspired   It is enduring marble
Carved in my heart and marshalls
Like bees to gather where it will
My errant senses visiting flowers
And all bright sources of the Divine
Nectar dropping beneath the stars
All blooms are holy and I seek
Dew everywhere that the Muse delights
In knowing that the Divine Form
Is indestructible even when Death
Scatters its shrivelling petals on the bank
And the black earth absorbs its own
White marble gleams in my heart
While the quick cells decay
Neither Lethe nor Styx nor Acheron
Nor the River of Fire in the mouths of men
Ever will melt the white-flamed frost
Of my tears and the tears of my Beloved
Or the vine-purple song of our mouths
The Muses are always dancing and the air
Each one of them breathes is itself
Brief Memory made divine and immortal
On marble they write in our hearts for ever
Though we sleep for ever dumb beneath marble.

Berlin, 1964

WEIHNACHTEN

er ist gewaltic unde starc
der ze wihen nacht geborn wart

In the deep valley
Dew drops from heaven
In the brain and belly
The paths shall be even

A Virgin holds Sun and Moon
In her two hands
There will be peace soon
In all the lands

A child is born under a star
Kings and shepherds greet him
A cool white nenuphar
The moon receives my hymn

I sing the dust on the moon's rim
And the gases of the sun
Great wisdom is in them
Though my praise be done

For the stag wanders in the wood
And the unicorn is stilled
Over the scrambling mud
Go footprints of a child

Berlin, 1964

THREE SONGS

for Benjamin Britten

I

Where is now the wandering stag
 And the drunken friendly faun?
The prophet wrapped in his woollen rag
 And the hare that lives on the moon?

Where is now the peeping dryad
 And the serpent in the brush?
Whose are these voices in the wood
 That bid me roughly 'Hush!'?

The forest's full of uniforms,
 The deep lake is still;
The wind-flowers seem to cry 'To arms!'
 And the harebells ring the till.

II

You, man, going down the road
 Have you got a soul?
A jewel gleams inside the toad –
 My heart's a glowing coal.

You there, lady, warm in furs
 What's in your soft breast?
Is it a kitten that gently purrs
 Or a tigress in your chest?

III

I hang my sorrow in the air
    From a rope of cloud.
Upside down it swings there
    While I laugh aloud.

I kick the earth with a hobnailed boot,
    The sky-god bares his teeth;
My sorrow dreams like a trailing root
    In the bright stream underneath.

The rocks are hurled about my ear,
    The storm rips at the tree;
My sorrow's tossed on the point of a spear
    But it still hangs free.

Berlin, 1964

WINGED AMOR PAINTED BLIND

and suckled by Aphrodite

Not milk, but bitter tears, my barbarous child, thou'lt suck!
Thy eyes plucked out, I give thee dart and bow
For being God of Love so art above the intellect
With blinded eyes thou'lt go
So gentle thou shouldst ne'er behold
Civilisation and its woe
But know
Voluptuousness
That's greater and more old.

Berlin, 1964

MONDAY MORNING

I

I look from the daffodils to where a shelf of books
Gathers the imagination in the shadowed past,
The calf-bound brain-cells blooming in the dark
All seasons, as the light of a mind illuminates them.

Why should I take one down when the daffodils
Spread light in the living brain-cells? Why require
Illumination out of the dark while the sun shines
And the ducks and the waterhens are diving in the park?

II

Perhaps there are no realities and the sweetness of snow,
Like sugar, is a theorem of shapes in space;
But the cubes and the hexagons know where to go
Because they are space, bent round itself and ordered
Like the single thread in lace...

Berlin, 1964

CLAIR DE LUNE

O blessedness of the ice-ray
And the ray from the sunlit deep

For the sun lies deep in the ocean
Tonight

The cold squid moves in the undertow
In the dark the electric monsters go

The shearwater paddles the air
And the Crab wanders through the sky

You who are clothed with flesh on the threshold
You who were naked under the moon
The moon has given you clothes

You stand in the cloister petalled with roses
Where the light is of ice and the darkness is of the depths

And your voice is a silver thread

Berlin, 1964

ELEGIAC

Heartsease of bird-song, overarching trees,
The silent whirring gnats – forgotten geese
Cackling where the last farm stops before the woods –
The long day goes by, so long, so brief –
A summer afternoon of flutes and violins,
Notes of Vivaldi or of Bach recalled
When shadows lengthen in the dreaming park:
You threw your book aside – watched a beetle crawl
For hours up a single stalk, or mused on Troy
Or thought of how Plato must have heard these birds
In terms so different from us and yet not different at all;
Then all at once you heard that spaniel bark
And it was supper-time. What if the bell of the Evangelical church
Signals midnight and you are still there
And the beetles gone in their holes and the birds stilled?
The Little Owls flit from oak-tree to oak-tree
Possessed of these natural alleys of space
You did not suspect before, and the sedge-warbler
Fills up the empty staves left by blackbird and thrush;
The earth goes on its path round the sun
And the moon silently revolves round the earth,
And the seasons and birds follow these pointers like the two
   hands of a clock
That are never quite in phase at the end of the year
Or beginning of spring; but they sing,
And the seasons return and the time seems unchanged
Each solstice or equinox. We grow older, it's true –
Die back like crocus or hyacinth when our cycle is done,
And we are wrapped and put away, withered, into the dark
And it seems like an end. But the children play in the park
With knucklebones, spinning-tops, whips, and in autumn
Collect fir-cones. And the flutes and the violins
Play on in the mind of the poet who lies in the grass
Every summer, watching a beetle, thinking of Troy,
Though it is never the same poet. The fixed stars
Are moving really, and the whole Galaxy turning

Round and round on its own axis agitatedly
Like the spinning ball of the earth – it was born
Back in time, grew in its true proportions,
And will wither away like a cloud formed in the morning
From dew and the dawn-moisture till it bulges huge in the sky,
But evening sweeps it gently away into the dark...

I look gently on lizards and helpless tortoises.
They are part of our past, and I think of the long ages
We have come through since the Cambrian dawn
When the first sponges and fish willed themselves on the sea
Imperceptibly, only five or six revolutions
Of the Galaxy, back in time from the present.

You throw the tea-leaves in the sink, turn on the tap
To wash them away – whirlpools and swirlings, linear streams
Like fleets of meteors rush from the corners,
Spiral nebulas race on the edge of currents
Throwing out straggling arms like the spark-trails
Of Catherine-wheels or swastikas, and the individual leaves
Are sucked from the edge till the pattern gets fainter and fainter
And eventually disappears; wide spaces of clear water
Expanding in transparent wave-circles in the middle
Where the tap-water drops, the waves returning
From the walls of the sink in vertical bores,
The leaves swept into constellations persisting a moment
As long as the contrary forces balance each other –
Globular clusters, outsize leaves stationary a moment or two,
A half-dozen leaves dancing around each other
Frenziedly in a minute compass, or amorphous clouds
Of thousands of leaves rushing to and fro but the whole
Maintaining a single appearance for a while
And the average density is constant. For a time
The whole star-sky is there in the chipped sink
– You pick out the patterns of vibrant leaves
Unaware almost of the water's unseen lines of force
That make the sodden clot of leaves into a universe
Till the pressure's altered and the pattern is broken up
And the whole mass washed down the waste-hole...

The dust in a sunbeam, smoke from a cigarette
Lit by the sun forming long streaks and hooks
Till it gathers in a level stratus under the ceiling,
Undulating gently   Then somebody opens the door...

So music in the air, or intelligence
Clusters, or forms a rarefied cloud
For an instant in time
And things seem significant, perduring

Till a barbarian army crosses the border
And civilisation is swept away

But the nightingale goes on singing
And the beetle
Climbs

And Alcman sings
And the cicada
Scratches his legs...

Berlin, 1964

MISSING A BUS
for Elizabeth Sewell

The time goes by. I'm talking to myself.
The birds and bushes speak. And language,
Which has sprung from them like finer stuff
Hangs over streets and walls and doors
As if an atmosphere of mist or cloud
Were Nature breathing; stones and animals,
Fish in their aquaria and streams, and trees,
Insects and lizards and domestic mice
Stilled for a little spell and uttering words
As I observe them...
The lamp-posts bend down to me and speak
And the trees' lower branches, finch-filled,
Prattle of draughts and rain. On summer nights
Moths fly in through the windows full of news,
With scalloped lemon-pale wings with narrow bars,
Swallow-tailed with long questioning antennae
And gleaming crystal eyes...

My life's a dialogue with Nature –
Cats talk to me, birds sing habitually
When I am listening, and the wind
Is always grumbling or gently sighing.
I reply in my own way, dumb for them,
But talkative, alone at all hours...

Sometimes the magpie rattles late at night.

I sleep; and sleep is energy. I dream.
And when I dream I'm thinking still
But with a depth that's different but as great.
Day's casual thoughts become the night's obsessions
When Nature tells its actions over again
And conscious thought becomes a dream of learning.
The wild valleys are full of signposts, and the hills
Are wound with pathways that are leading somewhere
Away from these dead ruins...

The landscape speaks under a hollow moon,
And time that's full of learning runs backwards to the groves
Where ochre-painted men speak dazzling fables
To the dark circle of the tribe...

They speak and they are Nature speaking
For the first time articulately,
As they perform what Nature has performed before,
Through language and the body, operating on Nature,
Interpreting Nature and yet subservient to it.
A first philosophy out of the springs of Science
Where what men do is a rehearsal of natural force,
An attempt not merely to control but to *be*
Earthquake and meteorite, volcano and the storm,
The moon's quarters and the sprouting seed –
So that softness and fertility may rule the earth
And the sky's angers be changed into fields of gold...

And now I wake, and everything is alien to me –
The chest of drawers that seemed a smiling face
Guards clothes that are no part of me
Until I go out on the street to talk to men,
This bed-post like a sentinel can be dismissed,
The door that slams behind me, just a door...

I came out of the gritty earth long since
As now I rise from sleep, put from me my encumbrances,
Deny my very provenance, and strut
Into a world in which the world's excluded
And only artifices are observed at all.

The flowering almond by the garden gate
Reminds me that I'm late;
Slow moving forms rippling the still fishponds
Beneath the neighbours' talk of *bonds*,
And the sparrows' barbarous cheeping
Gives way to the sound of weeping;
And bloated pigeons' gutter-capers
Fade beneath – the morning papers.
A newborn infant starts to squeal –

Something's wrong, I feel –
The crocuses have gone back in their corms.
What's Love but correspondence of these Forms?
The big-eyed pansies in the flower-beds
Shake their heads –
'SOUTH AFRICA ACCUSES REDS'
'CUBA PLANNING TO ATTACK US'
– Lord! I've missed the bus.

The time goes by. I'm talking to myself.
The birds and bushes speak. And language
Pours out of sky and tree.

I think – 'Ten minutes, and I'm free
To smell the pollen on the aimless wind
And hear the blackbird call his kind.'

What's Nature but the poet's mind?
O You, whom the storm refreshes...

Berlin, 1964

'FALLEN SIE LANGSAM'

I'm falling slowly in the night

The rain has fallen and the wind has dropped
The lime-trees in the street are silent now

From nowhere
Falling again to nowhere

Snatch a few kisses   Listen carefully
When the nightingale breaks the silence

Drink of the grape as long as the grape
Endures
And the artificial lights illuminate
The corners of eternity

Through the long shadows I am falling
In a night that is perpetual
Where all the living sleep

Berlin, 1964

DELPHI

Temple of womb and dolphin
Delphi of Muse and mice
Cypress and pine-cone – sunlight!
And the Greek guards playing dice.

Berlin, 1964

BLIND HOMER

ἐξ ἀρχῆς καθ᾽ ῞Ομηρον ἐπεὶ
μεμαθήκασι πάντες – XENOPHANES

Blind Homer, sniggered at by the ignorant soldiery
Invented Olympus, propped among the mules;
And Greece exploded into golden flames, and Europe
Slowly grew out of his long hexameters...

Berlin, 1964

BOY RIDING
Dorchester, 1933

That day I was alone with clouds
And the hammering of the cob's hoofs
On the spongy turf. I thought of no one,
Not even God, or you...
We cantered over downs where rain was gathering,
Past dewponds and the stationary sheep
Who hardly stirred themselves to look.
Their world was centred on the grass,
Mine in the rushing clouds. I thought of them
As they would be when night diffused into them
And their white consistency would be obscured,
Dissolved in that neutral darkness pricked with stars;
This white and azure of the coloured day
Ebb into dimness that you can't define,
A depth you cannot measure, and shades
That seem to change and yet remain the same;
That smoky grey, that carborundum glow
Suffused with Prussian blue and peacock green,
A light that's grey and blue and green at once
And yet not one of them, not even a light.
There are no shadows in the dark, the trees
Are blocks of black lumped on the indefinite
Skyline, and the sheep are merged in sepia hedges.
The clouds are higher than the clouds of day
And moon and stars shine through them
Easily, and night is full of voices
Like the day, voices that interrupt
The pummelling of hoofs, the thighs' continual grip,
The rider's cloudy thoughts; voices without a face,
Without a word, that seem to shriek
Of buildings toppling like these clouds,
And of a darkness as immeasurable
And colourless as night without a star,
Filled full of voices, faces, proclamations – words,
That have never known these coloured clouds or night.

Berlin, 1964

ANALOGY

So on the lip of being
You meet the lover's breath but not the lips
Themselves, and there is darkness at the edge
Of knowledge, but the wings sweep free
And air is rushing, when light lights up the tree.

Already the peace of sleep is creeping in autumn
But you may learn to entertain yourself
With everlastingness before the long year ends,
Sail your frail bark of knowledge through the dark
On a light invisible thread
Which lets you travel where the footpaths fade
On the bank, and the tree casts no more shade.

Berlin, 1964

LEAVING GERMANY

I shall not be here much longer.
Is it a sort of death
Makes me indifferent to things long familiar,
To wishes and needs that used to be so much stronger,
As I draw my last breath
And the month bleeds away as though dying of haemophilia?

I shall not be here much longer.
My life moves in the dark.
My wounds flow in this place but the long train waits.
In the mountains snow congeals. I shall be younger
Soon when the larks
Thread the descending slopes and their webbed song opens
    the gates.

Berlin, 1964

DREAM SONG

In the castle cats are singing
Frogs discoursing in the well
Crows reciting verses
While the drunkard rings the bell

In the courtyard someone's reading
While the wizard casts his spell
Also there's a Lady laughing
While the drunkard rings the bell

I am there and you are there
We hear a madman's yell
But the Lady keeps on laughing
While the drunkard rings the bell

Venice, 1965

VERSES WRITTEN IN THE SAND
for W.H. Auden

In this circle that I've dráwn
I place the gentle ox's horn.
My life's all worship, praise and prayer –
I do not mourn, I do not care!
Geometry was born in sand –
The new moon irrigates the land –
I who when enthusiasm
Shudders in me, note the spasm –
Write down intuition wet
In bold figures like a debt
With a circle round it, – pace,
Sensing all of time and space,
Up and down the room of life –
Till I balance Love with Strife.
These equations that I solve
Endlessly in words, involve
Contraries and opposites
Multiplied by my five wits –
Solutions various as the swarms
Of my many Protean forms –
Only resolved when man becomes
Quotient himself of all his sums;
And Nature, like the gentle ox
Gently draws him in his box
Like a schoolboy's answer, at random –
Quod (right or wrong) *est demonstrandum:*
And She trims her lovely horns
Or dims her circlet in the dawns
Other children will awake to
(Whom She's the eternal snake to);
And they'll draw upon the sand
Circle and line with trembling hand
As I do in extended play
Murmuring each blessed day
Praise and worship, hymns and prayer –
Full of mourning, full of care.

Venice, 1965

IN THE CAMPO DE LA BRAGORA

'Sleep, sleep, with thy broken keys
    Till Pilate wash his hands' –
The time is cracked and memory flees
    Bright afternoons of other lands.

What were thy once-tuned strings,
    Childhood and fluting boy? –
Mornings of swift protecting wings,
    Noons flecked with joy.

Blindly the hunter bat the twilight scours
    In the dark enclosure of the Square;
Green fissured bronze rings out the hours –
    The crowding ghosts halt on the stair.

Barbarian night creeps on the town.
    The Councillors sit late.
Tiresias has rent his gown,
    And the sentries closed the gate.

Venice, 1965

THE GOLDEN CHAIN

I lay in fetters linked with bronze,
 I begged a gift of the White Dove:
The silver chains that bind the swans,
 The golden chain that binds my Love.

The Dove said: 'Go to the Lake,
 And take a withy in your hand.
Look on the sky and air, and make
 A magic circle in the sand.

'Within the circle plant a seed;
 Wait for the Tree to grow.
Look on the sun and moon, and heed
 Word of neither friend nor foe.

'You'll see the mountain-tops rise up;
 You'll see the earth turn into fish –
The deep lake seem a crystal cup
 In which you'll dream your chafing wish.

'The fish will jump like silver birds
 Out of the crystal bowl;
Sprout legs and dance, and utter words –
 Words that will be your soul.

'Take all the words and write them down
 On the leaves of the growing tree;
And let the starlight like a crown
 Light up the leaves' calligraphy.

'And read again, and read again
 The words the green leaves spell!
And they will be the silver chain
 And the golden chain as well.'

       Venice, 1965

GIRL PAINTING

You took some empty, watery, colourless space
And placed some pink and blue to make a flower;
Light-green for stalk, and emerald at the base
For grass, black earth – but *magic* made your shower;
Which rains transparencies of light and dew
And sunbeams full of pollen none can see;
It seemed that everything was there – but You,
So feminine, add dabs of brown – a bee.

I knew that touch was right – your white gauche hand
Directed by some force we dared not name
Paused in its course to contemplate the land
Of light you'd made – and wonder whence it came;
I stood and looked, gushed – '*Liebling!* Oh it's grand!'
And rushed out of the house to choose a frame.

Venice, 1965

THE RIVER

When the cool stream flows beneath the violet night
And all the birds are hidden in the trees,
The pale moon scales the retreating darkness
And lights the steely surface of the flood.

Like life the river flows, all averages,
The ripples and the whirlpools seem to go
Like individual men through history, rapid
And meaningless as any gust of wind.

Venice, 1965

FOR EZRA POUND'S EIGHTIETH BIRTHDAY

SAN TROVASO

You walk alone along the road like God,
Grey-bearded, ancient, like a mad old king;
And you proclaim with absent-minded nod
That you've lost interest in everything.

LE ZATTERE

Becalmed, old man, step out upon the rafts
And start your marvellous journey once again!
Each day the world is new, and new bronze shafts
Drive new Odysseuses around the brain.

LA DOGANA

Becalmed upon what rocks, old man,
Are you bewitched and stay?
The hot Mediterranean intoxicates your brain
And the white dolphins play.

GIUDECCA

A gull stands motionless upon a buoy –
Old man, you seem to float upon great waves
Far out from the abandoned coast of Troy
And farther still from all the abandoned graves.

Venice, 29 October 1965

NIGHT RESONANCE

Lapidary and water-clock
The deep night's lucubrations
Ululation of hoopoes
And tongueless nightingales
The noise of distant jets
Airlocks in water-pipes

A lone singer in the Square
Paraphernalia of the humanist
Etymologicon, vocabulario
The crude rhymes beating in the head
Quatrain against clepsydra
Writing against the dead

Venice, 1965

VENICE IN WINTER
for Gitta in Berlin

The clouds obscure the island and the church
And the cold sea is streaked with grey like mud;
Dark cypresses (but not a single birch
As in Berlin), edge the Venetian flood.
Follow the Lido with your wind-swept eye –
Long needle of the land that threads the sea –
Where white gulls in the stormy distance, fly
Past lonely gardens and the last green tree.

You wouldn't think the citizens would dare
To venture out upon the streets below
With all this frosty dampness in the air;
But when night falls you'll see the scarlet glow
Of braziers roasting chestnuts near the Square,
And sweet potatoes in Sant'Angelo.

Venice, 1965

INTERIM

Somewhere along the way I seem to have lost myself
Or someone else has lost me.
I have no occupation or home, and I live
Under stars, under bushes, in a sweet vagabondage.

Far from the old pathways, the old retreats
And the meadows where once I lay chewing a stalk of grass,
I find myself from time to time now in cafés
Where there is vile music and cigarette ends pile the floor.

Here I read cheap cast-off editions of the classics
And waves of mild ambition wind up the hours.
But I am waiting for someone to find me again,
For someone who knows my name and the scar on my left rib.

There are many tendernesses in this loneliness.
I feel sometimes that someone wants to speak to me
But it is not that person I lost in retreating smoke
When the blue tiles of a church tower began to fall.

When the sun comes out I turn over the pages of my book
More hurriedly, and pay my bill and go out.
But the streets are full of strange people always doing the same,
And there is no face my eye rests on with pleasure.

Perhaps it was when I was away in a long dream
When a white unicorn was roving the woods
And I joined in the joyous hunt for a week upon end
That my true friend disappeared and my house fell into ruins.

But today I shall visit a little temple on the far side of a field,
A pagoda of sunbaked bricks with a golden spire;
I shall make some vows there and count over my hopes
And lay a bunch of wildflowers on the disused altar.

It may be that in the gloom of that deserted place
I shall see the face that I am looking for,

Or that those well-known eyes will recognise mine
Or speak as they once spoke in another country.

But I have fears that one day they will find me curled up
In a basket-chair in a roomful of unread books,
And the telephone ringing, and the door-bell ringing,
And fate calling aloud my name, but I do not stir.

And they will take me away to a small country house
Where the knives and forks are chained to the breakfast-table;
And the face that I love, the face that I sought, will visit me there
But I shall not recognise it then.

Venice, 1965

THE DEAD THEATRE

I remember still:
he was travelling to Ionian shores,
to empty shells of theatres
where only the lizard slithers over the dry stones,
and I asked him: 'Will they be full again some day?'
and he answered: 'Maybe, at the hour of death.'

GEORGE SEFERIS, *Memory II: Ephesus*

I have taken the wrong way and am riding an ass;
I think I have an ass's head but there is no mirror;
We are going slowly downhill towards nowhere,
And the backcloth is not even moving.

There are a myriad faces and bright lights that flare,
But I can only see the stars and a painted pine-tree
And the sharp stones on which my ass's hoofs go crunch,
And I hear nothing but the creak of axles.

There is no one else on my road, though I have in my pocket
Twenty-five invitations to tea from well-bred young ladies;
I lament the impossibility of normal means of communication,
And no one thing seems to be completely intimate.

It seems to me that I was once young
And that there were actual things I could feel;
There is a tree with canvas oranges, and a signpost
Also of canvas, but the arm is blank.

A little later on there will be applause, but my journey
Will not end till the curtain falls down;
There will be much moving of effects, and my donkey
And I will be hurriedly cleared away.

Of my next part I am not yet sure; the lines
Have either been lost or are not yet written.
I once was a soldier with a gun and a slouch-hat
And could smell the intoxicating stench of the midday jungle.

I think that now I am nothing at all
And that I am going, rather slowly, nowhere.
My pockets are stuffed full of illegible papers
And my ass's ears are of paper too.

Outside in the night there are motor-cars screeching at crossroads
And the traffic-lights flash on and off;
Khaki figures move rapidly across jungles
And there is a loud noise of grenades and machine-gun fire.

Someone is reading a glossy new declaration
To a faceless audience equipped with multiple earphones;
Twelve different languages are available from a single switch,
And they are rebuilding the Uffizi in yellow plastic.

I myself am indifferent to these themes of reconstruction.
My mother at eighty-six is dying in an old people's home,
Where she hangs head downwards like a bat
From the branch of a lightning-struck pine-tree.

To visit her I have to climb parallel bars
Like the bars on the walls of a large gymnasium;
But the walls are the walls of a massive theatre with boxes,
And the pit is crowded with uniformed men and women.

Outside on a small beach a dark green Rolls Royce
Is stuck in the sand and abandoned;
Upstairs in the second gallery there are many corridors
And the seats for the last performance are all reserved.

All the branches have dry rot and the bars come away in my hand;
The pit seems dark down below and I know I am falling.
Pegasus with long ears and a long-eared rider
Is tumbling out of the clouds and no one is even laughing.

The great theatre is full of actual people
Going on actual journeys officially.
Their papers are all in order, they have no questions,
And I am completely indifferent to my fate.

Venice, 1966

FROM A HOSPITAL WINDOW

A vast holm-oak tree
In the hospital garden

A carpet of shadows
Under the tall straight trunk

Earliest dawn   rust-coloured stipplings
On the silver-green leaves

The silence is absolute

Everything still
In the hospital garden until

A small child in a red jumper and red pants
Runs over the new-mown lawn
Looks up at the tree and with tiny arms
Embraces it

Firenze, 1966

MNEMOSYNE

Sea-foam, flower of prolific ocean –
Mnemosyne...

                  out of the Night
The Dawn that is the heaven's bride –
A god that blows forth flowers from his mouth
Beyond the senses' knowing

Mine are the waves of endless memory
Each image in its place in lovely order
The multifoliate robe of Kosmos in the soul
Ripples and ripples with the alphabets
Of every ancient science, every sense

I stand aside to let the seasons pass

And ecstasy, that threads like pearls
Our origins and presences and ends
Is like the first wild jonquils of the spring
That shimmer in the wind and sun
Upon a lonely island no one knows
Drawing the swallow transports out of Africa

And every clod and every grain of quartz
Gleams like the infinite stars
Answering around the universe

London, 1967

SPLITTING THE CENTURY

                              ... are you cold Byzantium?
Our house is empty, you are dead
And Rome is full of Turks

Each day's a century in which the smashed glass on the floor
Glows like red phosphorus ground to mash

The Red Guards and the Tartars charge
– Invincible horde of poster-heroes
They'll sweep up everything –
All the decrepit glass of Venice
– And drop it after Attila
Into the Lagoon

Do you mind, you petit-bourgeois drunkard and your girl?

There's no form any more and anything will pass
The needle's eye for the majority

Almost the firing-squad, icy and cool,
Would be preferable to these hot Dog-days
Sweltering in Manhattan or Venice (Italy)
Doing and caring nothing

Caring requires courage

A mist is forming on my eyes, Byzantium
I'm deaf to all the shouts

Scribble a little
Dribble a few contemptuous complaints
Through the tart saltpetre in the wine
And horse-hoof Parmesan

The next half-century's on the march
Red Chinese cavalry are landing on the moon

(I took a picnic there myself
Once, a quarter-century ago)

Well, – split the century!
Another eighth, sixteenth or sixty-fourth
Attila, Arthur, T.E. Shaw
Will come again perhaps
And who cares which?

My heart's wrenched out for the lost second,
Lost hour, lost day, lost week –
A horseshoe cast without a single spark
A two-thirds century
A stale croissant
Cold as the burnt-out stars
– Cross, crescent, sickle,
Hammer and anvil of years –

O Century I loved you once
You cherished me

The grand betrayal's in the head.
Dead souls, dead hearts, dead meat in cans...

O Aquileia, your mosaics,
Venice, your crusades...

We shall survive in paper
Wrapped up like Martial's fish
And stink, dear Century
Immortally...

Venice, 1967

NINETEEN TWENTY-THREE

On a bare hillside in a dream
The child lay

Strange music like that of bagpipes played

A stony path wound round the mountain-side

It seemed he had been on the other side
Long long before

That he remembered daffodils and birds,
Bright sunshine and a glittering lake,
Laughter, and this same music...

But now he heard the carter's shouts
Rasp in the crowded street outside
And steel tires crunch on the sanded stones –

All too familiar voices in the hall...

A grey and crumpled pillow
And garish trellis-roses on the wall

And darkness fading

Venice, 1967

MOSCOW THE THIRD ROME

The pagan Russian envoys to Byzantium
Entered the churches there in ecstasy.
When they returned they said 'We did not know
Whether we were in heaven or on earth.'

Hagia Sophia was brought to Moscow,
Vladimir pressed the new religion on his souls.
Then Boris Godunov sent out young Russians
To study in the West; – not one returned.

The Third Rome flourished under Peter.
The civil alphabet replaced the Church Slavonic.
And Peter Chayadayev went to Rome –
Came back with new ideas. He was declared insane.

They kill their poets or imprison them
In the new third pagan Rome.
I ask the tourists who return from there
'And is it heaven, or earth, or hell?'

Venice, 1968

PLUM-PICKING 1939

for Robert and Biddy Rowland

I set up a ladder long and narrow
(Parallel lines never meet)

I set it up in my youth
Against a plum-tree

I climbed into the sky and disappeared
In a cloud of blood-red plums
In the lovely vale of Evesham

Down below there were shouts
Of boys and girls from the camp
Swimming and playing in the water

But I was alone in the air

I was finding myself
In dusty twigs and green leaves

Looking up always
Precariously balanced
(When you look up
The sense of balance
Diminishes)

And there were the plums, the blood-red plums
Hanging like suns and moons
Glowing blood-red, or purple and green
In a sky of green leaves

The green ones hidden like stars in daylight
Waiting to swell and burst forth brightly
When their time should come

The circles of Heaven seemed near then
Earth very far below
The fruit itself seemed the fruit of Heaven

At the end of the day I descended –
(A day of muttering Keats's Odes
Ecstatically to myself, or humming
Arias from Mozart's Masses
Rejoicing   Rejoicing)

I descended

Five shillings for each hundred pounds of plums
Silver half-crowns like moons in the palms
Of a young boy star-struck

A month later I volunteered for the army
Rifle and bayonet, artillery, bombs

Seven years of unending railway lines
To and fro from the scenes of war

Seven years on the horizontal...

Firenze, 1968

IN A SUBURBAN GARDEN

Each man's a star that's travelling with us

Like holy images
He bears about within himself
Natural endowments
Which correspond with heavenly things

Poinsettias scarlet in the gloom
A last bird singing in the tree
The first stars prick the dusk
Lanterns to lonely man

Within his soul
Divine allurements
Trap yet set him free
In the nets of heavenly
Magic

Imprisoned in the dark
Unknown companions
Illuminate a little
His hidden purposes

He is always seeking companions
He is always seeking his hidden
His intellectual
Powers

For he is given
The five strong arms of his senses
Reason   and unlimited
Memory

Will to create and mind to execute
He bears within him
The soul being so construed

The form proceeding always – shape
Super-induced by man alone
In conscious intellectual labour

But memory alone makes things substantial
The world of solid things
Fades into unreality
When analysed by science
And there is nothing left to measure
But darkness in the mind
A flower's beauty

And worlds of vision open like the dawn
When underneath the tree the sleeper wakes
And like a child beholds glad day –
The Being of all beings –
The dawn-bird's everlasting cry

And a neat suburban garden
Lit by the stars or quickened by the sun
Assuredly is part of Eden

Venice, 1968

CHARISMA

Little poplar-tree,
Päppelchen!

You are like that sixteen-year-old
Daughter of sun and moonbeam
I see at dusk and at dawn

You are the white filly
Prancing in wide meadows
In furious winds

You are the hovering hawk
Chasing the rainbow

You are the sun and moon themselves
And the silken thread
That links their shining hands

Venice, 1968

JAJCE

Glad day embarks
And the gold sun mounts the sky

A little beetle crawls
Gold-backed
Over drying codfish
That hangs in market stalls

Hunger excites
The cinnabar of palate

Smoke cannot desiccate
The natural appetite

Sulphur, Old Nick and Paracelsus
Are nothing to the sun
Which lights the waterfall, and can
Materialise the rainbow
In this remote and river-rent
Provincial Bosnian town

Jajce, 1968

TSARA

Your tiny body like a little bird –
I want to hold it in my arms
And stroke your pretty feathers one by one
And kiss the golden down upon your neck

                    O it's absurd!
I want to kiss your little finger-tips
And feel your fragile bones within my grasp
To touch your slender naked toes with mine
And feel your delicate knees against me

                    And then your lips!
I want to press them ardently
On fire with – can it be with – love?
To hold your narrow hands all night
And all next day, until we grow –

                    Don't laugh at me!
Like root and flower, each into each –
I be your root and you my flower
And I your flower and you my root
Deep in the earth, yet leaping like the sun

                    Until we reach
Earth's centre and the Empyrean at once
Each buried in the other and yet flying
Like two bright birds free in the air
Calling like nightingales to one another –

Our bodies linked eternally by speech

                              Venice, 1969

MANUELA'S POEMS

Every night for nine nights Manuela appeared to me in a dream, and each night she spoke a poem to me. I had never seen her before and have no idea who she was. – P.R.

NIGHT THE FIRST

I am the rain
That rains upon myself
I am the thunder
That destroys my mind
I am the lightning
That blinds me –
Surely I am not so unkind?

NIGHT THE SECOND

Why do you ask me
If I am alone?
I cannot speak
To anyone at all.
Strangers are like blank walls,
Faces I know barred gates;
And every sound
               the click of a lock...
Nobody waits

NIGHT THE THIRD

The hours torment me.
I do not want anything –
Money, a lover's lips, fame,
Beauty for me, a husband –
It is all the same.
A house over my head
Is a house to die in.
Do not pray for me, mother –
Till you wish me dead.

Night the Fourth

Last night I prayed the Unknown God
For some Ovidian metamorphosis –
Rock, raven, touchstone,
Toad in Eve's ear
Or the abhorrent owl.
I woke this morning quite unchanged
And combed my long black hair,
Gazed in the oval mirror.
I am completely indifferent to myself.
I whom they say am beautiful
Am a dead narcissus in a pot –
'Don't water me!' '…water me…'

Night the Fifth

A pig that wallows in the mud
Plotinus says can be washed clean.
Dung-spattered bull tormented by the flies
Be milk-white, silken-soft like Jove
Tempting Europa on the beach.
Each morning when I take my bath
My body's beautiful and white –
But oh I have no appetite!
Wild strawberries or a peach
For me have nothing to teach.
I smoulder like a dying fire,
My native land the hearth.

Night the Sixth

People are kind.
They bring me orchids.
I have honey for breakfast.
The days consist of twirling clocks –

Ormolu, Dresden, Sèvres.
Honeydew melon, orchids, orchids, orchids...

Winter will bring chrysanthemums,
And the same twirling clocks...

NIGHT THE SEVENTH

My life's like sugar candy
It burns my mouth

I was suckled by wolves
Shall go take a bear for lover

In the afternoon

NIGHT THE EIGHTH

I was a happy docile child

One day I don't remember
I walked out on the hills
Heard music of the pipes
By a lake's edge

I live in a palace under the water
There are no sounds, no sights, down here

Everyone has gone away
To a great ball, they say

There are mice here
And I sit on a rush mat...

NIGHT THE NINTH

My real world
Is in your dream

I step into your mind
Out of my Sunken Cathedral

I breathe air once again
There are perfumes
Music and wild flowers
And live birds in the trees
Singing A Midsummer Night's Dream

My lungs are full of sodden incense
I am damp and cold

But in your mind
There is a big fire
And a red phoenix in it
Spreading his wings

I shall remember what I saw
In your real world
Which was my dream

And I shall try to be grateful

I'd give you all your heart's desire
But it would only make you unhappy

Goodbye...

Venice, 1969

NOTE: *I have never seen Manuela again* – P.R.

A BONE-RATTLE

The world is breaking up,
All by the nose are led;
The kids have been sold a pup –
Santa Claus is a Red;
Commerce and art a club
To sell love on an iron bed –
All that Plato and Thomas said,
Sand in the shoes of the world.

The world is consumed by time,
Time's in a hurry now;
What's the use of a rhyme? –
He drives a mechanical plough
And the poets' feet are lame,
Their wits are dull and slow;
All that the Sages know,
Sand in the shoes of the world.

Beauties survived from the past,
Things taught in academies;
Bulldozer and sandblast,
Scorn for the Parthenon frieze,
And eloquence disgraced;
Art become do-as-you-please;
The eternal verities,
Sand in the shoes of the world.

Painting's a way to show
Things that we do not see,
Neutral things that we know
Are mere irrelevancy;
Giotto and Michelangelo
Stuff for a Ph. D. –
Pythagoras, Pico, Alberti,
Sand in the shoes of the world.

And this is not the worst, –
Soul dies with the body, they say;
Such heretics were cursed
In Alighieri's day;
Now they are gratefully nursed
By usury's cold sway;
All things that are not clay,
Sand in the shoes of the world.

Venice, 1969

THE HOLY VIRGIN OF MILEŠEVA

Let language speak: it is the gift of man.
He hollowed it out like a reed-pipe
Placed in his mouth, and out of words,
Magical and musical and meaning,
Created Intellect from the first images.
History is hidden in his simplest words
Which pulse with life like limbs
Deep-threaded with invisible
Branching capillaries.

The first Adam did not name the things.
He knew the evident spirit
Of everything that breathes,
Knowing the life in stones and lakes and caves,
The hidden power of mountains, rivers, trees –
The definite voice of wind and waterfall.

Seeking to serve the wondrous powers
Servant became of every living force.
He feared, not loved, creation's forms.
Naming not things but powers.

We live, or think we live,
In worlds of naked things –
A waterfall a fall of water –
Rainfall and gravity combining with the drop
Or chance proclivity among the hills
Ancient upheavals randomly exposed.

And yet imagination longs to know
The long lost secret of the roaring stream,
The unseen spirit haunting the bright
Rainbow above the pool
Couched at the mountain's foot.

The beauty of a bird, bird's song,
The wonder of a plant, the flower's beauty,

Making the heart rage and intellect delight
In mystery solemn things inspire.

But from long habit we are dead
To all that's living save ourselves
And what ourselves create –
The artificial paradise,
The world of art.

But here, in the thirteenth-century church
The peasants cross themselves and kiss the ikons
Too rapt in reverence long to gaze upon
The Mother of Heaven's lovely face;
While the grave art historians wrangle
About an unknown painter's name,
A painting's date of composition –
Giving their names to 'Schools'...

I long to grasp the ikon's magic power,
To gaze intent upon the beauteous face,
The curve of cheek and nose and hand,
The long fingers' twig-like innocence;
To know the life behind the thing,
To see the thing in all its glory
And then to be myself
A part of that hid life

Names are exact, but nothing that's exact
Is worth a straw.
It is the life-blood, spirit, essence,
That roars like hurricanes or soothes
Like soft-plucked lyre-strings
Man's unknown heart –
Not names or physical exactitude
That give me power...

I ask, in reverence and in awe,
Adoring, yet in awe,
The blue-robed Lady frescoed on the wall
'Tell us your secret of eternal form –

Soft-eyed compassion that we never knew –
Tell us what Beauty is,
You who are wholly beautiful.'

I wait, breathless and agonised,
In passionate suspense,
The doe-eyes motionless, the tensed lips still –
And *words,* miraculous *words*
Echo around the church,
Silent as moth-wings or an eyelid's flutter,
Soft breath soothing perplexity.

She says:

'I am your image, you are mine –
Mother and son, sister and brother,
Father and daughter, belovèd and beloved,
Each in one another blest.'

I said:

'Stone Lady stuck upon the wall,
Is this your only secret?   Is your Love
Merely a mockery of me and all?'

O deathless pause, O vision in your eyes –
The first faint gleams perhaps of Paradise –

She says:

'I do not mock, I love with all my heart.
But how can I, my learned lover,
Tell of all people you – who know
Or ought to know –
I who am so remote, so fearful to you,
No other am but you, your deathless Self?'

But other voices filled the church,
The raucous clangour of the day,
And men with cameras came;
And with bright magnesium flame
They took Our Lady's photograph.
And one with hearty laugh

I heard exclaim: 'O man, well done!
Mary will like that one,
Not half.'

I looked once more,
But only saw
A peasant and her babe, a dark-blue scarf,

And I went out,
And wept for shame...

Venice, 1969

IN MEMORIAM

Osip Emilyevich Mandelshtam

The whole sky is a riot
Bicycle-chains of galaxies
Fires on the arterial star-roads
Factory on celestial factory a-smoke

Black dwarfs and white dwarfs
Red giants in squads
Pulsating beacons of the Cepheids

Titans and gods fall in the wake of history

And slow damp rain of tear-gas falls
Acrid and crass on miserable man

Venice, 1970

COLOPHON

I wove a web, a web of art,
A single thread, a seamless coat;
I'm sick at heart, I'm sick at heart,
I'm tangled in the words I wrote.

I sought to mirror all that's been,
I slither in a lake of mud;
I tried to sing of all I'd seen,
A tuning-fork of flesh and blood.

To mirror or to resonate
Natural creation's not enough;
The spirit is itself innate,
Bound in this fabulous stuff.

The song must sing the spirit of
Mountain and stone and root and tree,
From things inanimate strike Love,
On the anvil words set free.

It is the heart that celebrates –
Not brain or hand or eye;
The heart, that gags and binds the Fates,
And plants a garden in the sky.

Now I am bound in my own cords,
And I have built my prison-cell;
False words, false words, like petty frauds
Have caught me surely in their spell.

O heart, O heart, come let me out –
My spring tide's on the ebb;
Trapped in the maze of my own doubt,
I am the spider in his web.

Venice, 1970

SMOKE

'The way the English *professore* smokes! –
A tale to make an alligator weep!
His average is – he's not like other blokes, –
Ninety a day, and sixty in his sleep.'

They say he works in three unstaggered shifts
Without a break, – of reading, writing, *thought*;
Suggesting he's abused his natural gifts
For making money, pretty girls, – and port.

He smokes his way from 6 a.m. till 1
Reading old books and making lengthy notes;
Then cooks up *poems* out of all he's done, –
From then till 8, declining heptaptotes:

And all the while tobacco like a screen
Burnt to blue fibres in the kitchen air,
Drifts like the present past that might have been
A future perfect – world beyond compare.

From 8 to 3 a.m. he sits and thinks,
Blowing the azure fumes out like a beast,
Or like a broody owl or human Sphinx
Intent on riddles, in ferment like new yeast.

At 3 a.m. he rises to his feet
And wraps his thoughts around him like a cloak,
Close as a silent mummy's winding-sheet,
Ascends the stairs still in a cloud of smoke;

Removes his shoes and climbs into the bed,
Reads one last page of Wisdom for the night;
Thanks the great Gods for all the Sages said, –
Then stretches out an arm, – and dims the light.

And then this fumigated body sleeps,
And all its fumes like walls it thrusts aside,
Subsides in Soul, a harvest-mouse that creeps
At winter's onset, gently in his hide.

And then Illumination strikes that Mind –
The forms of all things that have been or will
Arise in the arena of the blind
Where all is bright and strange, moving yet still,

Eccentric, shambling like a living corpse
By day, a body spoiled of youth and blood;
By night, King of the risen tribe of Mouldwarps
Flinging apart the prisoning walls of mud, –

Naked among the eternal naked souls
He drinks dread secrets from the Sacred Fount;
Clear in his mind as brightly glowing coals
Beholds such Mysteries mortals daren't recount.

A single image, aeons past mere words,
Unfolds itself before him where he stands,
Beholding all of Wisdom's scattered sherds
Like a great Urn, the womb of Shadowy Lands;

And all the words of all the languages
Join in a single warp to make One Word, –
A giant molecule, that like a swarm of bees
Primaeval Gods in the first Kosmos heard

Descending slowly like a weightless Dove
On the first waters brooding like a World,
Until it burst, disseminating Love,
In boundless seeds like sperm or spindrift hurled.

And all the while that Soul beheld that dive,
That timeless spring from the Divine evoked, –
The body, in its drugged sleep still alive,
Its sixty winters of tobacco – *smoked*,

Till all that Beauty, darkened by the Dream
Fading like stars into the light of Dawn, –
He woke into the smoke of filmy *seem*,
Blind rags and tatters once again reborn.

Venice, 1971

UN PAÍS DE PAJAROS
for Octavio Paz

A country of birds

        Where's that?

It is a country
      an oil-painting
            a landscape
A place where we were

A precise memory inventing itself

An eternal
      birth perpetually
Perpetuating
      an eternal
           Path to the Paradise-Garden

The one true Country that
WE ARE

              Venice, 1971

I

There are woods and trees, dead sticks, and snow, and it is damp;
Against the dark background of the forest a man is walking.
He is tall in a long grey coat, and stalking, he slouches up,
He has a reddish nose, his tongue lolls like a swinging lamp,
His hat is black, and the mouth on his white face like a moustache
    is turning grey.
He is a rogue, or the Archangel, or Baudelaire, or God –
There's a red glow spread on the white of his face, and a pipe
    in his clay mouth,
Or perhaps there is not; a clod, I am alone, *yet we are four*
Irritable children sitting on the nursery floor.

II

This rogue or ruffian, tramp or beggar or God
Rolls like a drunk Russian, a vodka spirit by day,
Into this scene on the dark stage stark staring from winter's page
And sidles into the middle, shouts in his Irish rage:
'*I tread on the white, the Light; I tread on the black.*
Sand and the rivers, blow! Summer and sun come back!'
And the pools in the woods shine silver, the beech and the
    birch and oak, –
Red biddy the dawn has spoken: *What does it mean? We are four*
Shivering full-length snowmen square on the forest floor.

III

'*I tread on the white, the Light; I tread on the black.*
Sand and the rivers, blow! Sun and summer come back!'
And the white snowman in the top left corner of page
Droops, and he crumples a little, an old man grey in his age;
And the one on the left of me, (I'm on the bottom right),
Falls on his elbow, twists, – gyrates, – a rotating stick,
Dripping and dropping, deliquescent, sagging – a blubbing old
    statuette,

A white grey ghost on his elbow, a dying Gaul with the sweat
Running in blue-grey ripples off brow and shoulder and back;
And I feel like a sack collapsing, older, dwindling away... *We are four*
Dissolving ghosts in a puddle, wetting the nursery floor.

IV

The white of the glistening forest fades to a frosty graphite grey –
The top right-hand snowman has rolled on his Roman side – away,
To a pool in the mud and sticks, a pearly patch in the wove
Of a frayed old Turkey carpet we played on, just fifty years ago.
But strange, – like the dawn, – there's a shimmering roseate glow
Bleeding across the forest tinting the sky and the snow,
That turns to the red of blood, sweet wine that sticks to the paws,
Pink cheeks and shoulders, bare knees (all prone), – *Of course! We are four*
Bodiless babes that smoulder, – seeds on the nursery floor.

V

It seemed that our nanny or someone had played us some
    schoolmistress trick
Forcing us infants (poor kids!) to join in some giddy-goat game,
A vacuous dumb-show for tumblers who leap to a lifted stick,
A fatuous ring-a-rose nonsense, meaningless, always the same.
I groaned like a lump ground down, a weight on my shoulders
    like lead,
In squid-like invisible arms that twisted me slowly around
In a downwards expanding spiral, a sundial in autumn covered with
    leaves pale and dead,
Faint trace of the spinning aeon, the scattered hand of a clock...
Unresisting, sodden, I felt myself succumb – heard the voice of a
    ruffian mock,
An insolent Rimbaud intruding, a sneering and poisonous sound:
'*I* is another, you is *you, – contemptible imbeciles four,*
Wrestling and flopping defeated, fouling your nursery floor.'

VI

Fury, impotence, hysterical rage seized me then –
A formless deposit deprived of muscle and brain-power I writhed;
Recalling that action, – that *action*, prerogative owed by men
To their very nature was due, – 'We *are* not grass that is scythed!'
I struggled in vain, a handless and armless trunk, for sword, or for
    ink and for pen,
But no! Was I drunk? – only screaming, and icy and colourless
    wind, –
A frosty monotone pitch in my guttering eardrums sang;
Jaws locked, speech frozen – tetanus-speech, – and then the
    telephone rang:
The forest a livid vermilion, – the dawn wind lifted my hand;
And somebody said: 'Is it you?' *'Help me!'* I said, *'I am four*
Sprawling slimy abortions spread on the nursery floor.'

VII

The blood-red flame of the forest had paled to sickly green –
The voice on the line was pleading: 'I want to see you now.'
But how could I, – no more than a liquid vomit – a stain on the
    carpet, be *SEEN?*
Then words not my own, words thrown up like a meal, where my
    gullet once had been
Oozed from my mouth and took form: 'Meet me at twelve o'clock,
Noon midnight, equinox solstice, at the crossroads outside the
    town, –
I'll be there, don't be late!' and I put the receiver down...
And the sky was an apple-green, Earth a bright Angel, and – *zooks!*
The soiled carpet a meadow in flower, in seed and in fruit, *and we*
    four
Four tall golden stooks in the sun (and the threshers, gathering, come
With their ox-hide, winnowing fans and their flails) – *where there'd*
    been but a nursery floor.

Venice, 1972

THEOREM

How can one bear to be alive?
    Five hundred thousand things to do!
Solitary dreamer in a honey-hive,
    I dream of you...

The problem *is*, of course, – to *be*,
    In a dead world of waxen cells,
Not that there's monotony
    Even in insect hells.

To *be*, – it's no good buzzing round
    Doing as people do in Rome,
Droning of penny, shilling, pound –
    To build the honey-comb.

The honey comes from what you do
    Each rushing second, minute, hour;
Yours is the sweetness that is true,
    No matter what the flower.

The plants and trees are all in time,
    Petals and anthers ranged in space;
The *things* are simultaneous, – *I'm*
    Out of time, out of place.

For when I light on this or that
    I'm neither there nor am I here;
I can't see what I'm staring at,
    Though nothing's there to interfere.

The air is clear and I am free
    At any time of day or night,
To visit any flower or tree
    In sunshine, shadow, or moonlight.

What is it then that hinders me?
　　Why is it that I don't arrive?
– *I am a solitary bee*
　　Dreaming in a beehive

Where Time and Space have ceased to be,
　　And so there are no *things;*
I'm everywhere and nowhere, – *me*,
　　On imaginary wings.

Solitary but never alone,
　　Freeholder of the emptied soul;
Let workers say I'm just a drone
　　And drive me out the entrance-hole, –

Beyond the stratosphere and stars,
　　Past even humming nuclei,
My life which was hyperbolas
　　Is now a single *'I'* –

All sets and theorems put aside,
　　All space and matter lost to view.
Let insects make insecticide!
　　– *Honey,* for me and you...

Venice, 1973

THE ACT OF LOVE

The world's a vision   the neutral ground of things
Sexual and welcoming like mouths and arms

This rock (no need to kiss it like some neutered aesthete)

Beckons, its ruddy crystalline interior exhibiting
Like a woman talking, her body, hair, hands, mouth
Spelling the vision interiority reveals

Pegged to the rock a chain   The girl

The Dragon snarling

Disturbance in the air   and wings

Leila, our life has been too many words
Simple   agglutinative   syntagmatic
But always

                              empty words

This scene that reenacts itself
                              many times nightly
Many places   mornings   afternoons
Evenings and nights and the four seasons through

The neutral ground   description of the room

Objects   the alarm-clock on commode
The armchair by the bed
The wardrobe   curtains drawn

Of course the sheets turned down

After long day's Niagara of words
A hush
A candle burning

We talked as of the world and what's beyond the world

Two small lost souls conversing with the unseen
And with the third and unknown presence

The clock stopped ticking
Hours went by

Our words communicated through our finger-tips
Through unarticulated breath

After   she took her clothes off one by one
Placing them pensively upon the chair

Then talked with skin   the pulp of breast and lip
The armature of buttocks   legs and knees and feet

The hair beneath her arms green forest full
Of nymphs   the fountain and Armida's lair

Babylon's high-born virgins to the Temple come

And in her crotch   the mossy gate   vines overhanging

The fissure in the bony rock

                              You travel
The dark long tunnel of the darkest longest dream

Bodies reversed each going back in time

You enter through a lotus   part
The violet sacred petals gleaming on the sea
Of many oceans, millennia   life herself

Then enter through the heart while she devours

Her head hangs over the bedside   tense
The muscles of white neck bulging   mouth
A little open   tongue

Touching the upper teeth   the swarm
Of warm and heavy hair
A glossy mass   falls to the ground

Thick velvet curtains fall
Thud   on the Theatre of the World

Alone with nakedness

                              Grasp it
Eternal fugitive from absences eternal

All journeys now performed   all routes percoursed
Remain more journeys than before

The woman stretched full length upon her belly
The wisps of face pressed into pillows' cumulus
The skull concealed within the cloud of floss

Only the shoulder-blades   the saddle
Long rump   half-moons
Of pearly tidal buttocks
The musical cuneiform of slightly parted legs
And Venus girdles back of each the knees
Like quiet dells where suddenly the high winds dropped
And silence like warm water closed in on us

Soles of the feet   map of the moon and heart
The story of our souls written so clear
On those two gleaming pendent oblong mirrors

In which the Sun   the crescent Moon
Face of the Divine Child himself
The six directions   meet
                              all in a single plane

And the Reflection   rippling   goes down deep and deep
Into the unplumbed waters

Leila, sweet night, my fellow-voyager
Your narrow cusps of elbows row us now
Over the still soft silent cinder lake

The Sirens sing   and Lorelei   the Melusines
Pale effortless swimmers   draw us down
The height of Everest, it seems, into their Cities

This walking on the ocean bed through streets
Where Hammurabi's chariots rush and slaves attend
Naked their mistresses in linen robes
                                    The camels
Lurch and then kneel   the Bedouin armed with spears

                                        Cyrus
Has not yet come but will   and Alexander
Julius   Octavian   Agrippa   Antony

Pompey a smoking corpse on the deserted shore

And the Cathedral bells will ring   the sacred Doves
Fly from the gilded altar down the nave
And out into the Sun beside the Baptistry

And crops will grow   the green blades rise
And roots   like corals   swell beneath the earth

We see it all   crouched nakedness with nakedness
Here in Atlantis under it must be –
Under the Pacific

Alone on our Marquesas
Strange hands strange fruit strange figures in our minds
The rational the imaginal the true –
The intermediate lands

                                    Leila
Between your ribs honey is trickling into Time

Lie softly there

                 The Dragon's slain

Andromeda

Those chains around your arms and legs
Have fallen now   I toss them in the sea

And the tired dragon   limp in his pool of fiery blood
Turns in his sleep   his horny scales
Clinking like sparks and like the stars

Leila   full moon again!   You've turned upon your back

Leila   your face!   Astarte's opening lips

The white mirror of your belly now

All things I see in a mirror
The precious mirror I am polishing
Day and night these hundred thousand years

Full Moon   the Honey of your breasts

Your two lips torn ajar

Your Voice   a timbre   vibration   intonation –
Not yet Words...

Just measures

Life starts again   an incompleted Word

Venice, 1973

BROCK

*A poem of Quintilius's madness found inscribed on
the winding sheet of the corpse of a sacred prostitute
in the recently excavated Temple of Isis in Mestre.*

Sessile, a nomad,
Society, the professionals, would extirpate me
Did I not hide in my lair

A badger, they call me, the priests and the military tribunes,
The *rufuli*, rhetors and noisome rhapsodes,
The lying scribes in their scribaria
And the advocates in their short greasy togas

Of a Sabbath they will come together
And put on the tunics of hunters
And come to my house-door with logs and with sulfur,
And spinning the oaken stick
In the deep groove of my mother's womb
Set fire to birch twigs and then to the musty pile,
And so smoke me out

But I am wily – I have three back doors
(For borrowed wives and other emergencies)
And I know better than to leave my precious belongings
Unprotected in an empty house

Vamus

Into the virgin forests where badger dreams
Hang from the white undersides of the alders
By the side of shining nymph runs

And I sit by the light of a tuberose moon
And I whistle to the bats and flying foxes
Under a spreading oak-tree
Where the warm spring of Aponus, like Baiae
To the noise of forest-flutes
Bathes amenably and eases

The spirit Arthritis who has made long abode
In my strong retractable claws

I am Brock of the Virgin Forest
Not a two-legged ass in a city

Let them come with their sticks and their staves
Their tinder-boxes and their citations
Their lies and their purrings

I'll be gone by the time they arrive

Let them explode with hatred
Let them delight in deceit
And in the supreme pleasures of organised mediocrity

I'll be out in the brush
Where the ring-ouzel calls
And the merlin flies low over the rose-coloured flowering heath
And the good bees gather their loads of honey

In the evening I shall pay my visit
To my brother the old brown bear

And share, in the shaggy old hunter's
Trodden and comfortable lair

The honey we both have found
In the depths of impenetrable woods

Where the human sub-beasts won't come with their guns and
    explosives
And we shall sit on our haunches and crack
Nuts from the green hazels and filberts
And the spoils we have robbed from under the skirts of Aetna

And munch undisturbed

Fortune is Fortune indeed

The human beasts say it's a turning wheel

But in our good world we can manage well enough
Without such dubious benefits
As the crushing and crashing wheel

Bruin and I have excellent teeth
But the wheelwrights and carpenters and manufacturers of iron
    nails
The toothless fools
Have all gone to the barber surgeons
To buy a new set of grinders
Unfit to chew even a tender haunch
Of a young fallow deer
Let alone stag's dainties

And what do the idiots do
But cook it in iron pots
In slimy Capuan sow's grease

O *troia!*

Venice, 1973

ELEMENTARY

Who is the noise of waters?
Who is the breath of storms?
Who is the Earth, bright Angel?
Who are the Fire's forms?

Vocabulary of music,
The elements of speech,
Language of tomb and mountain,
Red shift of darkness, teach!

Wrapped in his ignorance, a man
Such questions well may ask;
The Potter breathes into the clay,
He spits, – fulfils his task.

He rubs red earth between his fingers,
Mysterious fluid flows;
Quicksilver balsam mingles,
Clay flares up in a Rose.

Victoria, B.C., 1973

ELEGY AT THE WINTER SOLSTICE

A poem of Quintilius's madness

Many good things are departing from me

Never again from this gold cup
The gold light at my feet shattered
Like the wild wind   joy shall I drink

5   Take now my Treasure   Leave me but Time

A kettle that's three miles deep   coral-encrusted
Perfectly formed   never-eroded crater

The prettiest one   that's now a beast
Hidden from the geologists

10   'Dark midnight' now   the end of an age

Harbour bottomless   anchorage none   a buoy
Floats on the flood

Late mooring...

Many foul beasts   great giants
15   I have overcome   (I was Athens)

More crowd in
In the Age of Wolves

Stone skulls of the monoliths
Unaided I smote   People prefer
20   Ballast and shards   mere makeweight
To living brain   the Bright River

With tinsel and tungsten   think to dazzle
Dim daylight's   blue dullness

Where is the marrow?

25 Have I not seen   the still deep pool of the sky
Million-point star-frost   sand-grained geometry

The jetty lake centre-cleft   great river running by
The moving belt of stars
Vedr itself in spate
30 Souls of the Dead   racing across the plains

Gems on a burnished bracelet
Twirled on a shining wrist

The Giants flee   it's only illusion

Back at the cedar *izba*
35 They wait for me

Smoke curls back   the winds enter
Flood rises   the treacherous Vedr

The ferryman mocks at the far side
Of the far-flung river

40 'Tell me your name
Ferry there's none   for folk that failed
Neither poachers nor thieves
Nor a man with parchments...'

'I slew the abominable   stone-headed giant
45 What did *you* do?'

'Fought on the All Green Island   five winters long
Conquered the cannibal man   the *wintego*
Gained there the love of seven sisters...

America blossoms'

50 'The hundred-legged darkness   hellfire   I slew
Tossed the dark eyeballs into the sky
Hung there two lamps   for day and for night

Spread there a million sparks
In each man's heart'

55 'Europe the lovely   deadly in sleep
Strongest of demons   I left dead
Wiled her out of her wit
Wasted her wand of magic

What were you doing then?'

60 'I sang my song to the growing seed
The green shoot   the sturdy stock

Laid gifts at the foot of the Tree
And the Tree gave out gifts to men

My bow was my drum was the world was me

65 What did you do?'

'I gave my gifts   to gold-happy bards
Good entertainers   content to obey
Placed them in colleges   clipped of their lack
They thrive there now   for their pains paid
70 As much as a lackey...'

'I was in Babylon   Jerusalem   Rome
Mammon I spat on   Babel outspoke
The Prophets praised   the Pharisees pitied

Nothing I wanted   though starved for bread
75 Wine had I in whirling words
Meat in my memory's measure

Seven men gathered to listen...'

'I was on Caucasus   there I enchained
A clown with a singing reed

80 Who should have had sword-haft
    Surplus or War   or the Thorn of Sleep

    The vultures are fat   the wolves fight free...

    What did you then?'

    'I slew the Wild Women   many a one
85 Witch-women   as werewolves they went

    I bent   each to my bidding
    Took my pleasure and ploughed

    Dark-shining flesh
    In a fair rut

90 Each vase of falsity   Base-hewn   I fashioned
    A four-square song   Bells rang
    In clear-veined Byzantium
    I met a man who took me North'

    'Much good may your following do you
95 Trade not use   teaches man sense

    Learning's a skill   like any other
    Earns a man bread   his fellows' envy

    Piecemeal pleasure   day by day
    Till the end come'

100 'Something I ween   for its own sake
    Is something worth   not given for
    Interest   exchange   or commerce

    What   I would not know   but the soul's joy
    String's resonance   or sparkle in the eye

105 Energy   leap of the toe and heel

Two sounds together sounding
Greater than the sum of them

Sweet hum as of honeybees

My bow is my drum is the world is me

110 Words alone   rhythm is energy

So little a body wants   but shelter   friends
Gift-bringing Memory's visitations

Light Time   Heat Sound   Draw lode
Love

115 It's much   in faith   that the Soul asks
Little enough though   in stuff and things

Love above all   though Love's a lot
Being from the Wolf sprung   and from
The People...

120 On snow moor   rock mount   wind acre
I learnt   *nawayēm*   soul   my friend
'*I wish to make my friend feel good*'

And what's a man   what marks him out?
He who follows a line   the Fisher Star   a thread

125 *Paths*

Hunter of Dreams   he finds them

Now
The Fimbul winter   "Dark Midnight"
The trail of broken treaties

130 Dark grows the sun   brothers fight
They fell each other

Axe time   Sword time
Shields are sundered

Wind time   Wolf time
135   Ere the world fall

Nor ever men
Each other spare

Day falls to night   Night swallows day
Snow stays   ice does not hurry away

140   The Spiders spin   but what they spin
Is each man's personal thread

The World's Cloak is changing from day to day

Little and little   some say
Rapidly others

145   But no man may know how the worlds change
Nor no god neither

Yesterday   only shapes   will there be
Tomorrow   ideas
Paths   will there be?

150   Shadow sticks   shadow sticks
           The Sun stands still
           And will

Light at his nadir
                    Don't despair

155   The wolves have taken my butterscotch

Remember the one-legged steadfast tin soldier

Remember the Bear'

                Cultus Lake, B.C., 12 December 1975

THE 'PROGRESSE'

When the long-legged rabbit climbed the short tree
And the loved serpent quadrupedly
In innocence espoused beasts and their mates
Were there not high places and a voice at the city gates?

Victoria, B.C., 1975

Notes

NOTES

ODE / 14
Friends, as well as critics, have found the title 'Ode' disturbing or unsatisfactory. I used it for a number of short poems at this time. If the immediate occasion was my devotion to the *Odes* of Quintus H. Flaccus, whose lyric metres I could never capture in English, subconsciously more archaic memories were at work, such as the Greek *ôdé*, song, *aoidós*, bard, and the Norse *Ódin*, as god of song. The mood of the poem, and so the rhythm, came as a result of hearing snatches of a famous oboe concerto of Cimarosa as I walked along a dirty street in bomb-scarred Battersea.

ODE / 15
This was another of the series of 'Odes' though the central image came from the work of the elegist, Sextus Propertius. The dedication to the late Norman Callan reminds me of the great and heartfelt debt I owe to my teachers in the English Department at Queen Mary College, University of London, notably James Sutherland, Norman Callan, and the late Dr B. Timmer. Callan and Sutherland both used to invite us students to write poems on a set subject as an exercise. I well remember my pleasure and surprise when one of my efforts came back from Callan with the remark: 'This is poetry of a high order. I would not presume to criticise it.' Our relations with our teachers were close and full of mutual respect. Nowadays I keep meeting students who tell me they don't know the names of their professors!

MELOS / 21
The dedication to T. W. Ramsey, the then President of The Poetry Society of Great Britain, is a small tribute to a man who helped me more than I can say in those early days. Ramsey ran a wholesale ironmongery business in the City and for all I know was an exemplary businessman. He was himself a poet of taste and skill and a man of considerable erudition as well as sensibility. I greatly admired his translation of Dante's *Paradiso* and eventually persuaded Erica Marx of the Hand and Flower Press to publish it with Roy Campbell's preface. Alas, he died before the book was finally printed.

The island in the poem might have been one of the islands of Brendan or Mael Dun which no doubt Ramsey and I discussed, but now, in retrospect, it seems to anticipate my many visits to Lundy in the 1950s.

THE RUIN / 22
Having left London to live quietly and write full-time in a cottage in Sussex surrounded by extensive woods, I became at a certain point acutely aware of an extraordinary sense, not of the forest growing around me, but of the trees rotting. One day I came on the corpse of a man in an advanced state of decay lying hunched under the ragged brambles. A few days later our house was burnt down. It was strange how so apparently idyllic a place so soon became for me a place of desolation. Having lived my youth near Bath, it was natural perhaps that reminiscences of the Anglo-Saxon *Ruin* should come to the surface in this poem. The 'gonfaloun' is the banner of the ancient Germanic peoples. Its various early Germanic forms

found their way into Provençal, Italian and Spanish as well as into Old English and Norse. The word conjured up for me something of the barbarity of the Dark Ages, the flight of the civilised Britons from the Germanic invaders, from the cities – which were left to fall into ruin – into the interior of the country with its inhospitable forests. The word later came to refer to the city ensign during the Middle Ages, and I had encountered it in Florence and Verona as well as in Provence. As for the word *oppidum*, which will be familiar to all those who had to read Caesar's *Commentaries* on the Roman conquest of Gaul, it is an ancient word, Etruscan probably, meaning a hill-stronghold. I had in fact just returned from a six-month stay in the *oppidum* of Cagnes-sur-Mer on the Côte d'Azur, the scene of the late life of Ford Madox Ford, and of Cyril Connolly's *The Rock Pool*.

THE ELEGIES OF QUINTILIUS / 24

It was in 1948 or 1949 that Robert Payne introduced me to Stefan Schimanski, the editor of the third New Apocalypse anthology, and at that time editor of *World Review*. When Stefan heard that I was on the way to Italy he quite casually asked me if I would try to do interviews with Benedetto Croce, George Santayana, Max Beerbohm and Ernest Hemingway. I was to get £5 for each interview if it was accepted, but no travelling expenses. It was out of the meeting with Santayana, then aged ninety, in Rome, that the Quintilius poems had their birth. Many small details, for instance the wolves in the Alban hills, came from Santayana's conversations with me. He had been impressed by the fact that since the devastation of the War wolves had once more started to live and breed so near to Rome. Many other details of the Mediterranean in general, and in particular of the 'Ligurian hills', came from my stay with Olga Rudge at S. Ambrogio near Rapallo the same year. Beerbohm lived only a few hundred yards away, and so it was easy to go and see him. The Quintilius poems are soaked in the light of the whole Ligurian coast, as I saw it there myself, and as I knew it from the *Cantos* of Ezra Pound.

I spent six months a year or so later at Cagnes-sur-Mer on the Côte d'Azur, a sort of extension of the Italian Liguria, where at one time the predominant language had been Ligurian. The second Quintilius *Elegy* tells of the poet's decision to take up residence in Provincia Romana, and the third describes his life there. While I myself was in Cagnes I spent much of my time reading Vergil and the Bucolic poets of Greece, and was especially absorbed by Jackson Knight's celebrated book *Roman Vergil*, which Eliot had lent or given to me. I also had with me the Ruddiman folio of Gavin Douglas's *Eneados* and read at it assiduously every day. I was at the same time studying Portuguese with my friend, the very beautiful Violante do Canto, the daughter of a well-known Portuguese sculptor. I recall with some amusement that just when we started to read Camoens I contracted a violent infection in one eye and had to go around with a black patch over it. Whether it was the town sewer which ran out into the sea where we bathed, or whether it was sheer auto-suggestion, I shall never know. During the same period I used to hitch-hike along the coast road, often through the enormous forest fires, to visit Richard Aldington at Le Lavandou and Roy Campbell who lived not far from there. Campbell was a splendid cook and his *bouillabaisses* with their scalding *rouilles* always seemed to combine with the numerous litres of rough local red wine to call forth a mass of reminiscence about the history and customs of Provence ancient and modern. Talking to me in the big flag-stoned kitchen he would be reliving the life he described in *Taurine Provence* and *Broken Record*, throwing in bits about Boethius and Cassiodorus, or curiosities from the Elder Pliny or Isidore of Seville. He described the bull-fights at Nîmes (Roman Nemausis) and the *naumachia* both of the ancients and of the contemporary fishermen, and would go on to read from *Calendal* or other poems of Mistral. Much of Campbell's information found its way into the versions of Quintilius. My own (and Quintilius's) eternal rancour against the bureaucrats and place-seekers was paralleled by Roy's tirades against the greedy, the timid and the mean. I suspect that virtually every image and phrase in the Quintilius poems was framed to chime in some way with some particular 'source', whether in the physical world as we observed and remarked on it, or in literature shared by us, or in Roy's or Richard's conversation. Roy was particularly well-informed on the history of the wines of Southern Europe and on the early history of viticulture in Portugal, and indeed was echoing Quintilius's own words as often as not, without knowing it. It was as though several minds across the ages combined in a single nexus and spoke with a single voice.

Tristia / 33

When I was about six years old I was told the old chestnut about how King Charles walked and talked half an hour after his head was cut off. I had already observed that the world is full of headless chickens walking around for brief spells, but that of course was not the point. The point our grammar teacher was trying to put over was concerned with *punctuation* – a lesson some of the editors in the larger publishing houses don't seem to have caught up with yet.

My copy of *Collected Poems and Plays of T. S. Eliot* (first edition, London, 1969) contains a number of errors in punctuation which have been carried over from earlier editions, and the same publishing house is responsible for erroneous full stops (that ruin the flow of the verse as well as its meaning) in two poems that are particularly dear to me – Wallace Stevens' 'The Final Soliloquy of the Interior Paramour' and Auden's 'Song' ('Deftly, admiral, cast your fly'). The error in the case of Stevens appeared in the first edition of the *Collected Poems* (London, 1945, though this is a printer's error for 1955!) and is present in the 1959 reprint, as indeed in the London 1953 *Selected Poems*. The error in the Auden poem appeared in the first London edition of *Nones* and in subsequent reprints, but mercifully was corrected in the Penguin *Selected Poems* (1958).

In the first four lines of the fourth stanza of Mandelshtam's 'Tristia' we encounter a somewhat different problem in punctuation. The Russian texts of the original Berlin 1922 edition of *Tristia*, the New York 1955, the Washington 1967 (revised and enlarged) and the Leningrad 1978 editions all have the same punctuation, which, quoting it in my own very literal version, reads as follows:

> *So let it be: the little gleaming figure*
> *Lies on the spotless earthen dish,*
> *Like the stretched-out skin of a squirrel,*
> *Stooping over the wax the young girl gazes.*

The Penguin translation has a modified version of this apparently authoritative punctuation, and reads:

> *Amen. The little transparent figure*
> *lies on the clean earthen plate*
> *like a squirrel skin being stretched.*
> *A girl bends to study the wax.*

Since Professor Clarence Brown, joint-translator with W. S. Merwin of the Penguin edition and himself an acknowledged expert on Mandelshtam, was also part-editor of the 1967 Russian text, this can hardly be an oversight. Indeed the punctuation of the Russian text lends itself to at least two possible interpretations. Is it the 'little figure on the clean earthen plate' that resembles the 'stretched-out skin of a squirrel', or is it the 'young girl bending over the wax'? Since the 'wax' evidently refers to the transparent or pellucid figure, and since a wax figure can scarcely be stretched (unless heated artificially), and since a young girl 'bending over' (*sklonyas'* – present participle) the wax and scrying (*glyadit* = she gazes, or scries) might well look like a squirrel's skin splayed out to dry, I take no credit whatever for using my common sense and equating the image of the stretched skin with the girl, not with the wax figure.

Clarence Brown, the expert on Mandelshtam, and W. S. Merwin, the poet and expert translator, refer to line 20 with the following note: 'Delia is the traditional name for the enamoured shepherdess of pastoral poems', and accordingly insert (on no authority whatever) the word 'shepherdess' where nothing in the Russian can possibly justify an image so untypical of Mandelshtam. My own translation is literal; I follow the original text I am translating – and so I am judged by the 'experts' as unoriginal and unimaginative; but at least I say what Mandelshtam says and do not mislead by writing in things he does not say.

In fact, of course, Delia is the name of the young married woman in the *Elegies* of Tibullus and I can't imagine her as a pastoral shepherdess! She seems to have other and far less innocent things to do! We find the image of her running barefoot to meet Tibullus in *Elegies* I. iii, lines 94–95:

> *Tunc mihi, qualis eris, longos turbata capillos,*
> *obvia nudato, Delia, curre pede!*
> [ed. G. Vitali, Bologna, 1942]

though this is an invitation and she seems to have run mainly in the opposite direction.

There are many other echoes of Tibullus in this poem of Mandelshtam's, including the at first sight very Ovidian 'Tristia' allied with the concept of 'Parting' *(rasstavanie)*, both of which are not infrequent themes in Tibullus *(tristitia, discidium)*, but the precise image of the girl scrying or of the waxen image is not to be found in his works. There are various oblique references to charms and spells, especially with herbs and other medicaments, as well as other forms of magic practised by agrarian peoples. Propertius III. vi, lines 27–30 is perhaps nearer, though certainly more savage and sinister, but in any case cannot be thought of as anything resembling that now unfashionable thing – a *source*. Delia probably had a whole row of squirrel-skin coats but there are no squirrels in the text of either Tibullus or Propertius.

To return to the confusion caused by ambiguous punctuation, I am quite willing to grant that while the method of scrying by pouring liquid wax into cold water and observing the resultant form taken by the solidified wax might well be referred to here, it seems to me less likely that the form taken by the wax would be like the 'stretched-out skin of a squirrel' than that the crouching girl should suggest that image. Thus while Brown and Merwin have altered the comma at the end of line 3 to a full stop, I have done the same at the end of line 2.

As for lines 23–24, I cannot restrain myself from a brief personal comment. At a first reading they might seem to be echoing some utterance of a pre-Socratic philosopher or perhaps a line of Sophocles, but later the echo of *Ecclesiastes* I. 9–10 in the standard Russian text (which is of course translated from the Greek of the Septuagint and not the Latin Vulgate) seems to swamp out any ancient Greek echoes. In fact, Mandelshtam's construction is closest of all to the exact order of the original Hebrew phrasing, but I do not know whether he read Biblical Hebrew or not. In any case, these two lines are for me among the most noble and solemn and suggestive lines ever written in poetry, ancient, medieval or modern.

THE RUINS OF MADÂ'IN / 34

This great national heroic elegy, composed by Khâqânî of Shirvân about 1180, celebrates the ruins of the capital of the last Sâsânid emperor of the Iranians at Seleucia-Ktesiphon on the Tigris in present-day Iraq, some five hundred years after its destruction in the Islamic conquest. The native Persian name *Madâ'in* (plural form of *medînat*) means literally 'the cities', and referred traditionally to the group of seven towns which grew together to form the capital, in the same way that the Seven Hills and their settlements eventually were linked to form the ancient city of Rome.

Khâqânî lived at a time when Iran was subject to the Seljuq Turks and might well celebrate the past splendours and greatness of an Iranian empire that had long since crumbled away into the rubble of history. His *qasîda* or *ode* is elegiac in tone and may be compared with the Old English so-called Elegy, *The Ruin*. The whole poem requires very extensive philological commentary. The three pages of notes by myself which accompany the translation in *Littack* no. III (ed. William Oxley, Epping, 1973) will be better than nothing for the reader with no Persian, but are quite inadequate. Several important works on Khâqânî have appeared recently, together with a far more coherent text than that which I had at my disposal.

'ASSES EN ONT SOFERT LA CUIVRE' / 40

I make no apology for the apparent obscurity of this text, which may be thought of as a poetic reaction to a reading of *La Chanson de Roland* in a mood in which the whole epic tradition from *The Song of Gilgamesh*, Homer, Vergil, the *Táin Bó Cuailnge* and Firdausi to the Arthurian romances seemed to be present. The English empirical and rational mind, not unnaturally, will seek to supply possible words or concepts for the unexpressed grammatical subject (I've tried to do so myself here, just as I have tried to identify 'a Lady' in my 'Dream Song'), but this would be to fall into the error of allegorising an essentially *symbolic* poem. That is to say, to reduce the irreducibility of the authentic symbol to the level of the sign, to the domain of semiology in the tradition of Peirce and his follower Thomas Sebeok, or to that of Freud and his Surrealist followers. While I do expect each part of a poem to 'make sense' I feel that the demand that a poem should be reducible to some kind of a rational 'meaning' is counter-productive – not of course that the poem should be 'meaningless' (far from it!), rather that the meaning of a poem (as opposed to philosophy or prose) consists more in the total impact or effect than in the result of epistemological and grammatical 'analysis'. A heightening of awareness and an evocation of a presence of more than the rational analytical mind can handle in any one moment is the sort of thing I have in mind. In this sense I feel more in common with a French poet like Bonnefoy than with the Oxbridge philosophers and poets in whose work 'a little meaning' takes precedence over any intensified awareness. Their concept of 'meaning' is post-Cartesian and diminished, mine has more in common with the earlier mentality of Old English *mǣnan* or the medieval Latin *intentio*.

With regard to the names of magical swords or other weapons, which I have always found very 'meaningful', I might mention that over a period of years I collected an extensive list of such names of magical weapons and their characteristics. Alas, this list is still in Teheran and the likelihood of my ever retrieving it and my many notebooks is minimal. The technologists and rationalists may well hold that such special weapons were named simply for their new and increased efficiency (just as we talk about the Sidewinder or Harrier or whatever) but they forget that the smiths were sacred persons, magicians or wise men as well as expert craftsmen. *Kavi* in Sanskrit meant 'wise, possessed of insight', a 'seer, sage or poet' and the root is connected with words meaning to see, look or *scry*, such as the Old English *sceâwian,* Greek *skopein* (to inspect the sacrifice), or German *schauen,* as well as with words for a smith, like Serbo-Croatian *kovač* and Irish *gabha* mentioned in my notes to Khâqânî's *qasîda*. Cú Chulainn's *Gae bolga* was surely something more than the sort of 'spear in the form of a screw' described by Diodorus Siculus (V. 30), if something less than Lug's lightning bolt itself, as suggested by T.F. O'Rahilly (*Early Irish History and Mythology,* Dublin 1946, pp. 61 ff). In the same way that the named magical weapon meant something more than improved techniques, so I think the poem 'means' more than its grammatical and lexical meaning.

As for the title, I have to confess to misquoting Bodel! I have deliberately changed the gender of *cuivre* from masculine to feminine. I leave it to the experts and the inquisitive to decide whether 'copper' (and so the sword-blade or arrowpoint), or the 'quiver', or simply 'care' or 'sorrow', is intended. Dictionaries of Old French and of French Etymology themselves fail to make this plain, however one reads Bodin! And why should not the exasperated poet get in his Parisian (sic) sniper's shot at the lexicologists who are sometimes as fallible, or at least as obtuse, as the surrealists?

Three Songs / 48
Many images, themes and echoes come together in this poem, but this is not the place for a commentary. I wish only to state the fact that the motif of the self-sacrifice of the Purusha in the *Veda* or of Ódin in the *Edda* was the central idea in my mind. There is also a conscious reference to the Sufi.

Winged Amor Painted Blind / 50
Platonic ideas discussed in Wind's *Pagan Mysteries of the Renaissance* and Vivian's *Shakespeare and Platonism,* as well as the painting in question, went into the production of this piece.

ELEGIAC /53
The occasion was a spring afternoon and evening spent in the park of Schloss Humboldt in Tegel, West Berlin. The Evangelical church was one near the apartment I lived in in Tegel. It sounded each quarter-hour with a Glockenspiel which played all too familiar Lutheran hymn tunes four or five times over, and nearly drove me to distraction!

'FALLEN SIE LANGSAM' / 59
Poems sometimes originate in chance and even apparently comic or anomalous circumstances. In this case I was walking (none too steadily I would guess!) along the Kurfürstendamm with some German friends at a late hour of the night when I stumbled and almost fell. One of our company jokingly cried out 'Fallen Sie langsam' and the poem simply 'came' then and there.

DELPHI / 60
The reader may well ask 'But why *mice*?' – More than one reader has accused me of taking advantage of an all too simple rhyme sound. The connection of mice with the cult of Apollo at Delphi is discussed in *Cinderella. Three Hundred and Forty-five Variants...* by Marian Roalfe Cox (Publications of the Folklore Society XXXI, 1893), and in Harold Bailey's *The Lost Language of Symbolism* (London, 1912). The pine-cone and the dice or knucklebones were among the playthings of the infant Dionysus. In some versions of the story Cinderella's coach is drawn by mice. The reader may like to compare similar themes in my 'Manuela's Poems'.

VERSES WRITTEN IN THE SAND / 65
In 1964, in Berlin, I had had several long and interesting talks with W. H. Auden on the question of incorporating scientific material in my poems. He thought it a good idea but was sceptical about the likelihood of success. He did however express his liking for this poem. Some of the imagery was suggested to me in the course of reading Plutarch's *De Iside et Osiride,* and Philip Wheelwright's fine book on Heraclitus.

THE GOLDEN CHAIN / 67
Cf. *Aislinge Oenguso* edited by F. Shaw (Dublin, 1934) or the modernised text edited by L. MacMathúna in *Feasta* (Samhain, 1970). 'The Dream of Angus Og' is one of the most beautiful of all ancient myths. Yeats's 'nine and fifty swans' must surely come from this source. The parallel with the number of Solomon's queens in *The Song of Songs* is striking. The version of the tale in a book of Irish folk tales published by Batsford around 1956 struck me as being much better than the one presented by Yeats himself in his *Irish Fairy and Folk Tales.*

THE DEAD THEATRE / 75
My friend Richard Burns suggested the epigraph which seems very apt, and I am most grateful to him. The images in the poem were all transposed from an actual dream.

MNEMOSYNE / 78
The image of the island with the wild jonquils is an actual memory of early spring on Lundy. The jonquils are only about four inches tall. They cast a marvellously

delicate perfume all over the extensive area where they cluster densely together on the exposed cliff top. The quartz grains are likewise the quartz grains of the narrow winding paths along the cliff-sides where the rabbits still breed in profusion, the island never having been subjected to myxomatosis.

MANUELA'S POEMS / 90
Some obtuse or unimaginative readers have doubted the authenticity of these poems as veracious dream-reports. I can only conclude that they flatter the inventivity of my conscious mind! I can only emphasise the absolute veracity of the two brief prose notes. The only alteration to the 'dictated' text was the substitution, some ten years later, of 'rains' for 'falls' in the first poem and the dropping of a comma in the last poem. The story that emerged over a year after the publication of these poems is material for parapsychology rather than literature and must be reserved for another place.

A BONE-RATTLE / 94
The Irish bards are described even as late as the seventeenth century as composing 'lying in the beds of booths' *(lighe a leapthaibh both)* 'the whole day in the dark', and there are extant several poems in which bards mock at the 'new sort' who compose while out walking or on horseback. This poem of mine, like many others, was written at the crowded bar of Harry's Bar in Venice! The fact is that the elaborate preparations made by the late bards for composing their purely literary poems represent a vestige of archaic magical rituals which had been forgotten by that time (see Keating's *History of Ireland,* written in the seventeenth century, and the striking description of the bardic schools in *Memoirs of the Marquis of Clanricarde,* 1722). Maybe we of 'the new sort' would do well to buy a sheepskin rug from the local giftstore and spend the night sitting on it before the high altar of some ancient temple in the hopes that 'inspiration' may come. Well, maybe...

THE HOLY VIRGIN OF MILEŠEVA / 96
If I have insisted on the precision as dream-report of certain poems I must here observe that in some cases, as in this poem, the memory of a very intense experience of another time and place reasserts itself, relives itself at some unexplored interface of conscious and unconscious mind. The poem just comes into being and grows in form and content with practically no conscious direction. Call it a daydream if you will, mere fantasy it certainly is not.

FOUR SNOWMEN AND A FIFTH / 106
This poem is a faithful dream-report. Nothing was put in that was not in the dream, and nothing that I could remember was left out. The central image is that of a page of a Russian children's book which had been familiar to me for fifteen years or more, and which consisted of four brightly coloured pictures of a snowman, arranged in the four quadrants. When I woke up, I was so delighted by the memory of this favourite old book of mine that I went upstairs to the library to get it. After going through the few dozen Russian children's books there I failed utterly to find it, and had to admit that the memory had been in fact created entirely by the dream, though I still could not believe it.

136

The poem was dismissed as opaque and incomprehensible by more than a dozen editors to whom I humbly submitted it in the early '70s, and yet audiences of schoolchildren and of people who are not literary students or experts have found it eminently comprehensible and *meaningful*. I've never had much time for modern linguistics and its attempts to inform us about what language is, or for semantics and its lamentable efforts to tell us what 'meaning' is. These eggheads, together with their fellow nestlings, the modern philosophers, keep telling us that words (not to say phrases) don't have meanings, they only have *uses*. They speak no doubt for themselves, but certainly not for *me*. In the unsophisticated days of our youth when we had never heard of structuralism, let alone 'communications', it was quite usual to hold that poetry is a form of communication. This has all changed now. The authoritative *Guida a la semiotica* [*sic*] by Omar Calabrese and Egidio Mucci in the Sansoni Università series (Firenze 1975), in its Glossario di terminologia semiotica, at p. 167, has: 'Fuzione (*sic*) comunicativa 1. Funzione dell'atto di comunicazione, compito primario svolto dalla lingua (Martinet 1960, Buyssens 1943, Prieto 1966). 2. Funzione propria della lingua quotidiana, che si realizza mediante la selezione di materiali usati, privi di ogni rilievo di novità, statistici nei confronti della norma (Circolo di Praga 1930). Opp. a FUNZIONE POETICA.' I can't say I'm much impressed by the amount of 'information' Mr Calabrese manages to squeeze out of the learned works of his colleagues, or by the low opinion he has of 'quotidian language'. The trouble of course is that the linguists never manage to break out of the charmed circle (crazy cyclotron?) of what *they* say language is, or for that matter, outside the charming circle of chit-chat with other linguists and their unspeakable wives. As a momentary antidote to their perverse, even satanic, *tantaferate,* I would suggest that Writing, when properly managed (as you may be sure I think mine is), is but a different name for conversation (Shandy 1760). It seems to me, who not seldom peep out of the magic thornhedge of language into the 'extra-linguistic' world, that this poem is a quite natural narration, as it were to friends, of a striking dream I had, even if it has been raised from the rustic tones of 'quotidian language' in Harry's Bar to what Dante calls the *vulgare illustre,* and from what he calls the *stilum comedie* to the *stilum elegie vel miserorum.* And this is precisely what the Florentine did with his own striking dreams (e.g. *Vita Nuova*, III) even getting a number of excellent replies in verse from friends like Guido Cavalcanti and Dante da Maiano. However, our *sem(id)iotics* think differently. Magister Calabrese, under 'Funzione poetica' has the following 'definition': 'L'enunciato è autoriflessivo, mira ad attirare l'attenzione su se stesso (Jakobson 1963). Mobilitazione completa e individuale di tutte le risorse formali messe a disposizione dal codice *indipendentemente da ogni intenzione comunicativa.* Le norme statistiche proprie della lingua colloquiale vengono stravolte da una realizzazione che ne sottolinea gli aspetti formali *senza preoccuparsi del contenuto* (Circolo di Praga 1930).' While most of this is sheer bunk I have taken the liberty of italicising the bits that are not merely bunk but also a mendacious travesty of all serious poetic practice, not to say common sense.

The reader at this point may wonder why I have expatiated on the linguists and semiologists instead of giving a note directly on the text of the poem. Firstly, I wished to draw attention to the fact that the 'experts' (? editors) found the poem either incompetent or unintelligible, and I wanted to suggest that this is probably because they have swallowed hook, line and sinker the rotten pabulum handed out as intellectual nutriment by linguists and language teachers in Universities over the past sixty years, and that this sort of semantic and semiological approach (broadly speaking, structuralism) represents a servile giving of comfort to those of the human race who are trying to set up the perfect slave-raider ant Kingdom on Earth. And secondly, I wanted to draw attention to a full analysis of 'Four Snowmen and a Fifth' by Professor Anthony Johnson of the University of Florence, which to borrow words ('materiali usati'?) of the earlier Florentine 'redundava la mia capacitade'. (See *A Garland for Peter Russell,* ed. James Hogg, University of Salzburg 1981, pp. 54–127.) Johnson states that his analysis is 'based on a structural-semiotic method' but in fact he completely transcends this approach, and unlike the semanticists fairly confronts the extra-linguistic facts of the poem, and even ventures to examine what rude rustic clowns like me would call the *meaning.* In our time, the study of language has been degraded from the Arts Faculty to that of the Social Sciences or Inhumanities. Professor Johnson is highly to be commended for reversing this perverse tendency and illuminating the text instead of fogging it up with tautological jargon. Structuralist method is in fact an admirable tool in its own right, i.e. for the study of structure, the articulation of the raw linguistic and phonetic components, but when it tries to explain the 'encyclopedia', i.e. the extra-linguistic, so-called real world, it is quite inadequate. Relying on it would be a bit like hiring a garage-hand or mechanic to act as a guide for a tour of the ancient monuments.

I am not in any way suggesting that all structuralists are fools and knaves, but only attacking those 'grammarians' who hold that 'meaning' is not dependent in any way on extra-linguistic factors. This sort of attitude has more in common with the typical trade union mentality than with any scientific attitude.

It is one thing for men to skin cats and another for the skinners to remake man in the image of the Norwegian ship's rat. If this is what our technological 'culture' has brought us to, I for one feel it's high time to leave this sinking ship.

THEOREM / 109

As a subjective lyric this poem obviously functions on the personal existential level, but there is a metaphysical level also, suggested at least by the employment of figures from mathematics – *imaginary* wings, *hyperbolas,* a *single 'I'.* If the last started as the 'single eye' of the Gospel according to St Matthew (plus an image from Khâqânî) it developed into the concept of a single, or integrated 'I' in the sense of *ego* or self, and then into the image of Aleph or the figure one. Hyperbolas may be thought of as pairs of corresponding curves which never meet or 'kiss' save in the unique case where they become straight lines and are superimposed on one another, as would be the case of the axis of a double cone, a form familiar to readers of Vico and Yeats. 'Freeholder of the emptied soul' is an idea developed from one of Meister Eckhart's greatest sermons (see *Meister Eckhart* by Franz Pfeiffer, 1857, translation by C. de B. Evans, London 1924, pp. 3–9. This is by no means the best English translation but it was the only one available to me at the time).

As in most of my poems there is also an overt social or political level too!

ELEMENTARY / 119

'Nous célébrons cette liturgie en l'honneur de la Terre qui est un Ange.' – Avestan liturgy for 28th Sirôza. 'La Terre est un Ange, et un Ange si somptueusement réel, si semblable à une fleur!' – G.-T. Fechner. See Henry Corbin, *Corps spirituel et Terre céleste* (deuxième édition entièrement revisée), Paris 1979, p. 31ff, and notes. The first edition, now a rarity, was entitled *Terre céleste et Corps de Résurrection* (1956), and presented the same material in a more poetical form perhaps, but the new edition is no doubt theologically and philologically more coherent.

ELEGY AT THE WINTER SOLSTICE / 120

At a first reading this may give the impression of a certain obscurity, if not obscurantism, a literary vice constantly attributed during my youth to poets as limpid and crystal-clear as Eliot and Pound. As Emerson said: 'a weed is a flower whose virtues have not yet been discovered.' 'Fate always keeps on happening' as Anita Loos remarked in her immortal *Gentlemen Prefer Blondes*, that dangerously Manichaean text of the classic 'twenties, and indeed Fate did happen to me in the summer of 1973 when my friend Herr Harigastl, the renowned cuckoo-clockmaker of Bollingen in Switzerland, presented me with a very ancient specimen of that noble art of the antique Rhaetians. I confess my mind was not primarily on cuckoo-clocks that catastrophic summer and I fully intended to hurl it down the mountainside, but something oddly impalpable bade me open the thing up first and see what was inside, apart from the cuckoo. Having established that the movement was genuinely antique, and indeed of a type quite unknown to the Christian era, my interest was somewhat augmented. It kindled even more however when I noticed that the unusual cedar box was lined with a crinkled and blackened parchment. On examination I identified the characters on it as being in a late Etruscan script of the type which was employed by the wizards and sorcerers of the Northern Germanic peoples until they adopted the Latin script in the late eighth century, when they became Christian – *creitin*, as their Swiss forebears had it.

Owing to my exacting duties at the University of Victoria in the period 1973–5, it was not until the end of the latter year that I was able seriously to study the ancient parchment. The precise stages of the decipherment would be out of place in a footnote to anything as worthless to the academic world as a book of serious modern poems, and must await the publication of my paper on 'Pre-Columbian North American Romano-Celtic' for which a famous International University has offered me an Honorary D. Litt., if I pay them the sum of £100 (other learned poets no doubt have had the same generous offer in the junk mail from India).

I shall content myself here with a few notes on the way in which this extraordinary 'poem' (undoubtedly by Quintilius) totally abandons the classic mould and in fact incorporates elements not only of archaic Scandinavian oral tradition but also echoes traditions and beliefs of the indigenous peoples of Northern Quebec province and British Columbia.

It is typical of Quintilius that he was not content to limit himself in a comparatively short poem like this to the mere meeting of two unknown exotic cultures well outside the Imperial frontiers, but that he had to introduce elements from prehistoric Greece and even Sumer and Ancient Egypt and India. For this unaccustomed purpose he had perforce literally to invent, or at least improvise, a diction totally alien to that of the classic Greeks and Romans, whom he had followed so assiduously in his more conventional youth. For this reason it was impossible to translate his lines with anything of that noble decorum which persisted in Western Europe even until very recently, and made it possible for our own poets, when approaching an exotic culture, to perpetuate the well-proven Latinate diction in, for instance, a poem about India with its

> *Distinguished elephants endorsed with towers.*

In fact, Quintilius's barbarous diction and his gallimaufry of vulgar Latin larded with words from Gaulish, Frankish and Gothic, not to say extreme Northern forms, gave the amazed translator a considerable freedom for manoeuvre. In any case the days of faithful verbal translations are long since past, and the academies and Foundations have instituted the novel dogma that the translator of poetry doesn't need to know the language he translates from and can simply express himself as he wishes, as long as he sticks to some sort of a 'modern' diction already approved by Creative Writing experts (who don't even need to know their own language, let alone that of some foreign culture). Such translations are known as 'Imitations', presumably out of immemorial respect for Aristotle, whom they've probably heard of from Northrop Frye or Harold Bloom.

Once I had worked out the general meaning of Quintilius's text (to generalise is to be a true scholar?) I was immediately struck by the remarkable consonance between Quintilius's estimation of his place in the cosmos, in history and in society in that distant and barbarous age (some experts might call it savage rather than barbarous) and my own evaluation of the situation of the *doctus poeta* (are there any such?) in our contemporary world with all its advantages of progress, higher education, abjuration of superstition, religion and the supernatural, with the concomitant substitution for the infantile idea of the divine, of the concept of *chance* as the unique and universal causation. In fact, the coincidences and the sheer synchronicity of the whole experience were so striking that if I had not been forewarned by Professor Bloom's sagacious study of the effluents of influence, I would have assumed a direct causal chain between this recondite text (which can have been read up to now only by myself in medieval and modern times) and the whole complex of recent research on catastrophism on the one hand and eco-systems on the other. I mention synchronicity and coincidence because it was precisely of catastrophe and ecology in their hypercosmic context that I had been reading during the autumn of that year, and the gradual decipherment of the obsolete Etruscan symbols seemed miraculously to illuminate and confirm all that as yet remained obscure for me in writings as different as De Santillana's *Hamlet's Mill* and Velikovsky's *Ages of Chaos* and *Worlds in Collision*. While certain extremely learned scholars at Simon Fraser University assured me that Charles Olson had said all there was to say on this subject long before Quintilius said it (though they could not quite remember just what he *did* say) I had ample and gratifying consolation from the wise men of the Interior Salish tribes (to be carefully distinguished from the Coastal Salish) who used to foregather nightly at the only beer-parlor in Chilliwack, and who were all deeply versed in the writings of the late J. R. R. Tolkien.

Line

1 For a precise description of the state of our contemporary society, see Eleanor Duckett, *Gateway to the Middle Ages*, New York, 1934 (2 vols.). Only ten days after my decipherment of this first line I received a letter from Professor George Watson, the distinguished literary historian and bibliographer, informing me (as though I didn't know it) that not only the world, but also the academic world, was 'already deep into the Dark Age.'

2 It may well be that Goethe's 'Es war ein König in Thule' can now be attributed to a source much earlier than those normally associated with this poem. However the 'gold cup' suggests the Celtic vessel of plenty theme, the cauldron. It is very unlikely that Quintilius had any gold cup.

5 Where Q. writes of his 'Treasure' one might be justified in suspecting a gnostic or mystical source, but the valuation set on 'Time' confounds any such suspicion. In fact a line from an early Scandinavian lay precisely echoes this one of Quintilius. Modern parallels are not unknown for such good sense. 'The cost of a thing is the amount of what I will call life which is required to be exchanged for it, immediately or in the long run' – Henry Thoreau, *Walden*. (Cf. 'We have to rely more and more, in the technological society, on the resources of the mind' – Pierre Elliot Trudeau). If Thoreau's statement is crystal-clear, one wonders just what the eminent financier means by 'mind'? The contrast well illustrates the points at issue in the Quintilian and the Eddaic flyting.

6 'kettle': Cf. Rhys Carpenter, *Discontinuity in Greek Civilisation,* New York, 1968. See passages about the bottomless anchorage of the island of Kalliste, known as Thera around 1000 B. C., later as Santorin. The 'kettle' is of course the *caldera.*

10 If the evidently conscious reference is to the Fimbul winter of the prehistoric Scandinavians, a secondary analogy to the 'dark midnight' of the Hopi should not be ruled out. Cf. J. Donne, 'A Nocturnall upon S. Lucie's Day'.

14 The transition from the prehistoric Aegean *locus* to the soliloquy in a predominantly Northern Teutonic context (cf. Dasent's *Northern Tales*) is effortless. Although plainly soliloquy it may also be taken to constitute the first section of the subsequent 'flyting' – the earliest known example of such a device in a non-Romance context in Europe.

15 'I was Athens': The identification of himself by the poet, a Berber of base origins from the unspeakable slums of Sfax (Hadramaut), with the culture hero of Athens (Theseus, as I presume) is not to be taken in the literal sense as so much vaingloriousness, but rather as an example of that *Verscheidenheit* without which the poet can never transcend the petty limits of his own personality and *hubris*. The concept of a culture *locus* like Athens necessarily evolves through many phases, from the primitive, as evoked here by Quintilius, to the historical as illustrated by its contemporary literature, to its reflex in later literature (e.g. Landor's 'Pericles and Aspasia'), to its exaltation on to the imaginal plane to a Utopia as in Shakespeare's *A Midsummer Night's Dream* (cf. P. Russell, *Paysages Légendaires*, London 1972, pp. 33–36).

17 Q.'s extremely vulgar Latin has *variculti* which plainly does not fit the context here even if it is construed as dog-Latin. In the archaic Scandinavian context, plainly it is a transcription of *vargöld*, 'time or age of wolves'. This seems more plausible than a possible *vargljoth*, 'wolf howlings'. The lack of culture in Q.'s time was indeed appalling and in many ways due to its 'variousness'. It was at first tempting to accept the seemingly Latinate word at its face value.

Q.'s inspiration plainly comes from some rudimentary knowledge of the Eddaic traditions though they could hardly have been written down in his day. Even so, his memories of Rome or Athens or Hadramaut, where *homo* was indeed *homini lupus*, can hardly have been much different from those of Santayana, or of Mandelshtam (in the Third Rome), with their animadversions on wolves. The translator himself has seen a wolf in Venice at a late hour of night, though it is only fair to mention the fact that his verbatim report to the International Association for the Protection of Wolves has been held up to doubt on the grounds that the observer maintained that the wolf was in hot pursuit of the poet Shelley. In any case, it is plain that wolves are with us to stay, whether in the Alban Hills or in our supermarkets and gift-shops, not to say the Foreign Office. Celtic etymology – and I shall shortly be publishing fragmentary evidence for Q.'s familiarity with the Celtic world – bears this out in a singularly convincing way. The German *Volk*, 'the people', neutered in English into 'folk', appears in Irish as *olc* meaning evil, rapacious, wicked. Obviously this is cognate with the Russian *volk*, 'a wolf', and the Sanskrit *vrka*, or Avestan *vǝhrka*, so identifying the root with the predominant class in modern society. That Quintilius was aware of this connection some fifteen hundred years before Karl Marx was born is surely noteworthy? Indeed I shall demonstrate before long from another Quintilian fragment carved in Runic letters on the tail of a maple-wood mermaid now in the museum at Cape Breton that Mr Al Purdy's celebrated lines

> *Tho we run to the edge of the world*
> *our masters would track us down*

– probably the best Canadian poetry has produced in the modern age – are in fact, though of course quite unwittingly, a word for word translation of a couplet – yes – of Quintilius, which permits us to claim the latter as the first Canadian poet. And we should bear in mind too that Mr Purdy's words were placed in the mouth of a Gaelic slave runner in the service of an early Viking band. I would suggest that the Celtic presence solves the whole problem (except of course on the political level which I am not competent to judge) and would even go so far as to maintain that Quintilius was making cranberry wine on Cape Cod before St Brandan set forth in his wolf's skin coracle and sailed for Cap Chat, P. Q. The evidence in a late author like Dante is of course interesting, but hardly reliable; but incontrovertible evidence of an archaeological, that is, a material nature, of Quintilius's actual presence at *Cultus* Lake on the other side of the Continent may persuade even the incredulous that Canada existed in the cultural sense before the establishment of the Canada Council. It should however be emphasised that the name 'Cultus', misunderstood by the early settlers around A. D. 1956 as having something to do with culture in the modern Canadian sense, is in fact a very ancient Interior Salish word originally meaning 'bear's excrement' (*cul*-toos).

22 'tungsten': not to be confused with the modern meaning of the metal used in electric light filaments. It means 'hard stone' (Old Swedish) and is employed here by Quintilius probably in the sense of the *skald* or bard's customary award. Just how lustrous or precious it may have been we have no way of

knowing. As is well known 'culture' is often equated with 'bread' and it may well be that Quintilius with his Christian *penchant* was unconsciously echoing the well-known words of Our Lord about giving away bread to the needy and undeserving. On the other hand it is also known that these 'hard stones' were an essential part of the ritual (of the *cultoos*).

29 When I first deciphered this passage I was puzzled as to whether it meant that the *weather* had become blustery or whether the *ram* (Aries) was in heat, but since the poem is about the Winter Solstice, the latter explanation seemed less likely. However, when I discovered that the river which waters the area of the Cultus was called the Vedder I realised that here was the first corroborative evidence for the remarkable journey of Quintilius to the shores of the Pacific. Striking confirmation of the verisimilitude of this passage was supplied during the actual period of my translating this poem, for the river Vedder rose in flood destroying several miles of roads and washing away the beautiful water meadows beside the Chilliwack Lake Road, so depriving us of fresh milk and cream till the following spring.

47 See F. G. Speck, *The Naskapi*, Norman, Oklahoma, 1938. See also the same author's 'Penobscot Shamanism', *Amer. Anthrop. Assoc. Memoirs*, I (1919), pp. 239–288.
   'wintego': cf. Old English *witega*, the wise man or shaman. In various languages of Labrador the word *witigo* or *windigo* is used for the solitary dweller, and represents the idea of the 'cannibal man', a sort of monster. Not to be confused with the *atceu* or *loup garou* of the *habitants*.

53 While the distant echoes of both Eddaic and native Indian mythology are hard to discount here, the 'million sparks' can only be a Manichaean icon.

63 'In clear-veined Byzantium' etc. Are we to take this as referring to Quintilius's starting-point? If the voyage of Q. to Labrador should seem implausible to positivistic humanists and others of the unimaginative, we may recall the voyages, no less than seven hundred years earlier, of Pytheas of Marseilles, who travelled the West coast of Europe, visited Britannia, Jutland, Orkney, the Shetlands and Iceland (Thule) where he observed the summer solstice. See also *The Vinland Sagas: The Norse Discovery of America*, ed. M. Magnusson and H. Palsson, Harmondsworth, 1965; and Louis Kervran, *Brandan le grand navigateur celte du VIe siècle*, Paris, 1977, and the extensive bibliography on early travel to America. See *Islandica*, vols. 1, 2, 24 and 38, Ithaca, New York, 1908, 1909, 1935 and 1957.
   There is no substantive reason why Quintilius should not have sailed from Tralee or Clonfert in a coracle, or from say Alet in what is now Brittany in a wooden ship of Phoenician type such as was used to transport tin from the Cassiterides, or even in a Celtic *ponto* of the sort described by Caesar in his *De bello civile*, or, much less likely, in some kind of a forerunner of the Scandinavian *drakkar*. M. Kervran claims to show beyond a shadow of doubt that the traditions of Celtic transatlantic voyaging ('le fond réel de ces traditions remontant probablement au IVe siècle – ou antérieures?') are in no way mythical. 'Que ceci soit mythique est certain pour ceux qui ignorent que les Antilles étaient connues des navigations antiques, Celtes compris'

(p. 176). He continues, 'En tout cas, ce Bran (ou Brân) n'a rien à voir avec Brandan, quoi qu'en disent certains auteurs, devant le docte assurance desquels on ne peut que hausser les épaules. Malheureusement, cette confusion se retrouve dans des ouvrages, par ailleurs assez sérieux. Pour ces auteurs, Brandan serait une fiction, une réincarnation de Brân qui se perpétue ainsi... Des Celtisants admettent que "certains détails peuvent fort bien ne pas appartenir à la mythologie, mais être un écho déformé de lointaines et audacieuses expéditions" (Arzel Evel, Ogam 1957).'

M. Kervran is 'Membre de l'Académie des Sciences de New York' so there is no reason to doubt his scientific and scholarly conclusions even where he forgets to cite his evidence or quote chapter and book in accordance with the MLA style sheet.

The fact that Q. in his remarkable *De umbris* demonstrates his advanced familiarity with the Venetic language and especially the language of the *matelots* (not to be confused with the later Breton *Ma'lo*, MacLou(p) – son of the wolf – better known as St Malo, whom some of the dark age chroniclers confused with Brendan, just as others confused Brendan with Bran) makes it all the more possible that Q. sailed from the N. W. Atlantic seaboard of Gaul. However, on the grounds of internal evidence I personally favour an entirely different interpretation. Since there is no reference to either the Veneti or Armorica in the poem and since Byzantium is clearly named, is it not more likely that Q. went to Canada via Byzantium rather than by way of Gaul? In the *Povest' vremennykh let* (ed. Likhachev, Romanov and Adrianova Perets, vol. I, Moscow–Leningrad 1950, pp. 11–12) we read of the *put' iz Variag v Greki* (the route from the domain of the Varangians to the Greeks) by way of the Dnieper, the Lovat, Lake Ilmen, the Volkhov, Lake Nevo and thence into the Varangian sea (the Baltic). Classical scholars no doubt will hold that since the word *Varangos* first appears in Greek in A. D. 1034 in the Byzantine historian Kedrenos (see *G. Cedrenus Ioannis Scylitzae Opera*, ed. I. Bekker (CSHB), Bonn 1838–9, vol. II, p. 509), the Varangians could not have existed before then. However, Varangoi or no Varangoi, St Andrew himself used this very route when he wished to return from Sinope to Rome, going up the Dnieper across the Baltic, and back along the Western seaboard of Europe, past the Pillars of Hercules and on to Rome (see *Povest'* p. 14). If St Andrew could think of returning to Rome from Sinope via Scandinavia and the Atlantic, why should not Q. go from Rome or Venetia (or wherever he was – maybe Ragusa or Dyrrhachium) via the Slovenes (then near the modern site of Novgorod), Varangia, Thule (Iceland) and on to Victoria and Cultus Lake in British Columbia (whatever the native names were then. That I would not know, but no doubt the Indian languages experts at the University of Victoria would know. One of them even told me that he knew the Polynesian languages as they were in 10,000 B. C., so they *must* know). Personally I see nothing in the least unlikely in Quintilius's North American voyage – it merely requires, like M. Kervran's scientific and erudite book, a little imagination and a certain *faith*, as well maybe as some Canadian Nationalism (M. Kervran is evidently a Breton nationalist and this enables him to dispose of all claims of the Irish in any field whatsoever as completely spurious).

To prove the plausibility, if not the absolute certainty of my thesis, I would suggest that scholars should seriously reconsider the etymology of the disreputably late word *Varangos*. That it was used in Rus' before the Greeks heard of it and in a sense quite different from that of 'the Imperial Byzantine guards' has been demonstrated by V. Thomsen (*Ruska rikets grunnläggning genom Skandinaverna*, Stockholm, 1882) and it is still generally (*sic*) agreed (see Sigfus Blöndal, *The Varangians of Byzantium*, translated, revised and rewritten by Benedikt S. Benedikz, Cambridge 1978, p. 4) that the derivation is from the Old Norse *var*, meaning 'confidence, vow of fidelity' (cf. Italian *mafia, camorra*). The proto-Norse for these armed bands of merchants (confidence tricksters?) would be **varingr*, related words in other Germanic languages being Old English *waergenga*, Longobardic *waregang*, Old French *wargengus*, etc., i.e. people who have 'ganged up' (see *Glossarium Suiogothicum*, Stockholm, 1769; vol. II, pp. 1069–70).

On the other hand in Russian the word appears as *Varyag*, Old Russian **varegu*, and up till recently has been understood to mean Scandinavians, Balts, Goths and later even English, who were *foederati* of the Russian princes (Thomsen, *Grunnläggning* pp. 103–6). A more recent view, however, is that although the word comes from the same root, it means rather a 'common liability', 'one for all and all for one' within each gang, a situation which sounds familiar, certainly plausible, to the modern mind. (See A. Stender-Petersen, 'Zur Bedeutungsgeschichte des Wortes *Vaeringi*: Russ. *Varag*' in *Acta Philologica Scandinavica*, vol. VI (1931), pp. 27–30.) These and other learned theories are discussed eloquently and at some length in Blöndal, op. cit., p. 4 ff and include the rather unlikely explanation that 'Varangian' comes from the same origin as the modern Icelandic *vaeringi*, which means 'cheerful', 'lively', the feminine plural *vaeringar* being employed in the sense of 'discord', 'quarrel', so that in Old Icelandic *vaeringi* must have meant at first 'quarrelsome fellow'. Benedikz-Blöndal refers here to B. Halldorsson, *Lexicon islandico-latino-danicum,* ed. R. Rask, Copenhagen, 1814, and S. Blöndal, *Islandsk-Dansk Ordbog,* Copenhagen, 1920–24, and while I would not think of doubting the learned Septemtrionals, my own consultation of *Teach Yourself Icelandic* and the Oxford *Dictionary of Old Icelandic* has not been as reassuring as one might have hoped. All I can find is *Vaering jar* = Varangians, *vaerr* = snug, comfortable, peaceful, *vaeru-gjarn* = fond of rest and comfort, none of which help much.

As there aren't any Old Scandinavian dictionaries in the Department of Germanic Philology in the University of the Veneti here, and as my own copies seem to be on permanent enforced loan to Ayatollah Khomeini, I've no way at present of extending my research into this vitally important subject, at least until I can get enough money for a bus fare to nearby Patavium. But it may well be that this is not even necessary, because in spite of my profound respect for the *eruditi*, my own meticulous enquiries into the text and personal psychology of our author (who, mark you! was not only learned but also a *poet*) leads me to propose a far simpler derivation of the word 'Varangian'. *Obviously* it really comes from the Old Norse *vargr* = a wolf, which word is cognate with Old English *wearg* = a villain, scoundrel, felon, criminal, outlaw (see Bosworth and Toller, *An Anglo-Saxon Dictionary*, Oxford, 1980 (1898); *Altenglisches Etymologisches Wörterbuch* von F. Holthausen, 3te Auflage, Heidelberg, 1974; and Grimm, Jacob, *Deutsche Rechtsalterthümer*,

2te Ausgabe p. 703), and so ultimately identical with Latin *vir* or Old Irish *fer* = a man. If this be so – and who could possibly doubt it? – then Old English *weorold* = the world *(Zeitalter)*, the age (like Mandelshtam's *Vek*), humanity, and Old Icelandic *vargöld* = the age of wolves, would be the same, ánd Q.'s apparent obsession with wolves would merely make him a sort of humanist before the Age of Humanism (that is, the period of the rise of Nationalism) and maybe the first man (wolf) to say '*mit den Wölfen muss man heulen*'. Incidentally the Old Icelandic *varg-dropi*, which supposedly meant an 'outlaw', might well have had a meaning more akin to the proto-Salish *Cultus* than one might savour from Zöega or Cleasby-Vigfusson-Craigie or even the excellent Sigurthur Orn Bogason. Q. was a hunter born, and as the *De Vomitorio* incontrovertibly demonstrates, had a nose. Whatever the etymological confusions involved in historical linguistics he certainly could tell wolf-droppings from horseshit, not to say know when the right moment had come to quit the *Cultus*.

The question remains, now that his tomb has been discovered, how he transported himself from the North West Pacific to the heartlands of the Sasanian Empire and was assumed to a professorship by the corps of Imperial neo-Platonists in exile from Attica.

On the face of it, a text purporting to show Quintilius (born c. A. D. 370) not only among men of Old Scandinavian stock and tongue, but also engaged in an Atlantic crossing, must seem irresponsibly anachronistic. If the Vikings did not enter history until they exported themselves to other peoples' territories in the eighth century, it doesn't mean that their ancestors did not exist – somewhere at least – and presumably had some sort of a language? In an age when the history of the human race has been put back from a mere 4004 B. C. to some three million years ago, it would seem churlish to dismiss the idea that an upstanding Roman like Quintilius might have gone North and West – whether trading or proselytising it matters not – and slipped across the 400 miles from Iceland to Greenland and then across the narrow straits to Baffin Island or mainland Labrador. The scientists anyway tell us that it was much warmer on the Arctic Circle at that time. After that, it was just a matter of walking. I very much doubt that Quintilius covered as much ground on foot from the Atlantic to the Pacific as he had tramping between the bookshops of the major cities of the Roman and Persian Empires.

I would like to take this opportunity to acknowledge gratefully the assistance of Dr James Hogg of the University of Salzburg, who kindly provided photocopies of Dr Imre Boba's *Nomads, Northmen and Slavs*, Slavo-Orientalia, Monographienreihe über die Wechselbeziehungen zwischen der Slavischen und Orientalischen Welt, The Hague 1967, Band II. The Muslim sources about the Varangians and the *Bahr Varank*, as the Arabs called the Baltic Sea, have provided useful confirmation of some of the translator's hypotheses about Quintilius's land route to the North.

Timi og klukkustundinn alone will decide the matter.

65 The hard-headed interlocutor's rudimentary economy and mindless view of the human condition and the *skald*'s rejection of them seemed to chime with two quotations I copied into my notebook around this period. Q.'s actual words are *negotium* and *gaudium*.

'There is no fundamental difference between man and the higher mammals in their mental faculties.' Charles Darwin, *The Descent of Man*, London 1871, Chapter 3.

'The Whites caused an upheaval in the sub-Arctic economy when they encouraged the Indians to produce for *trade* rather than for *use*.' Peter Farb, *Man's Rise*, New York 1968, p. 58.

88 'Love's a lot': the word used is *sors*. I was even tempted to translate 'Love's a *deal*' but I felt this might be misunderstood, especially by the academic confraternity.

The working of Quintilius's mind is not easy to follow here. My impression is that he has connected etymologically the Venetian form of *lupus* = wolf – *lovo* – with various forms of the Germanic and proto-Italic developments of the IE root **leudh*, which take on the meaning of people in the sense of 'heer- und dingberechtigte Mitglieder des Volksverbands' (Kluge, *Etymologisches Wörterbuch der deutschen Sprache*, Berlin, 1975 [1883] under *Leute*). While this would be unpardonable error on the part of one familiar only with the common vernaculars of this century, for one like Quintilius familiar with languages and forms which were extremely ancient even in his day, there may well have seemed to be plausible grounds for connecting these words for the commonalty of people, with their banal expectations of the rights and perquisites granted to hangers-on, with other words of the same derivation which approached rather closer to the dignity, nay sublimeness, of the concept of *love*. While the banal words meant no more than people, folk, men, *wolves*, in the case of the Greek *eleutheros*, the Latin *liber* = free (in Old Latin the form *loebesum* is equivalent to the classical *liberum*), and *liberi* = children (not to be confused with *libri* = books which never were free), a man as uninstructed in modern philology as Quintilius might be forgiven for connecting these words with the roots from which the later word 'love' and *Lobe* = praise originate. Even Aristotle wasn't much good at linguistics or etymology. I suspect that Quintilius, in a world in which 'love' was equated with *cupido* (from which our word 'covet' developed in the Middle Ages) thought of 'love' all too often as connected with rapaciousness and the root **raub* = to snatch, pillage etc. The latters 'r' and 'l' do sometimes get confused, and in the absence of scientific laws of sound change which were only established (and rather shakily, let us recall) some millennium and a half after his death, Q. may surely be pardoned for confusing people, wolves and love to the point of identifying them as a single phenomenon. Today of course with the advantages of modern psychoanalysis (etc.) we can just dismiss this as acute paranoia and the whole problem is solved.

In fact Quintilius is not the only learned person to get mixed up between wolves and men. The distinguished Marxist critic Gordon Childe insisted that human society originated in the same *syndrome* as the wolf pack and even today his theory seems to command great favour, especially amongst government sociologists, industrial psychologists, admirals, generals, schoolmasters and trade unionists. Unlike Quintilius though, these latter do not seem to have given much thought to *love*. And of course, if Quintilius was in the lands of the Slavs, as I believe him to have been, his Venetic love = *lupo* might well have assimilated the Old Slavonic form *ljuby* of the modern Russian *ljubov* = love, as with the case of the troubadour Peire Vidal whose *domna* was actually *luba* = she-wolf, and who himself was hunted through the woods like a wolf by his feudal lord. So perhaps there is something in it after all.

If the connection of 'love' with 'wolf', e. g. Friulan *lōf* = wolf, *love* = she-wolf (see A. Zamboni, *L'Etimologia*, Bologna 1976, p. 58), is obvious, that of 'wolf' (Church Slavonic *vlŭkŭ*, Russian *volk*) with 'people' (German *Volk*) is even more so, but the parallelisms with 'robber' and 'thief' are perhaps less evident. In fact the attempt to establish parallels seemed at first something like *iungere volpes,* an absurd or improbable undertaking. Quintilius certainly knew a wolf from a fox. He had spent much time wild-boar hunting in the hills and valleys of Friulia. On the other hand Quintilius was not unacquainted with *voluptas*, and this penchant of his may well be the key to this complex problem. The *k* in Greek *lúkos* and in *alōpēx* would seem to point to 'people' (*Volk*) rather than 'love'. But as Quintilius well knew 'Amors l'a pris par son volage' – love is a thief, a robber of hearts, is it not? A very flighty thief in fact – 'le faucon *vole* la perdrix'. Here there may well be a further connection, for in Friulia *vōl* actually does mean 'wolf', though it in fact derives not from *lupus* but from *lŭpŭlus*, and is employed now only in the name of the parasitic plant *Cuscuta europea,* which is known in the hills round Udine as *vōl*, but further West along the Tagliamento River as *arba lova* (i.e. *herba lupa*) or simply as *lova*. English-speaking people call this ravening bind-weed-like vine by the rather unpoetic name of the 'dodders' or 'quaking grass'. The evolution is from *lŭpŭlu*(m) $>*lōbol>ōvol$ ('l' misinterpreted as definite article) $>*ōol$ (intervocalic 'v' falls) $>*vōol$ (typically Friulan prosthetic 'v', cf. Venetian *vovi* for Italian *uova* = eggs) $>*vōl$ (Zamboni, op. cit., pp. 58, 63–4, 69, 132).

Thus the identity of 'wolf' (*vol*) and 'theft' (*vol*) is proven. The Irish *faol* (= a wolf) seems to bear this out, though the feminine *faolchú,* rather than being cognate with *volk*, may in fact consist of the components *faoil* (= wild) and *cú* (<dog). C. Buck is dubious about the etymology (Carl Darling Buck, *A Dictionary of Synonyms in the Principal Indo-European Languages,* University of Chicago Press 1949, p. 185) as is Walde-Pokorny (I. 213). The fact remains that Irish *faolchondacht* means 'wolfishness', and here the connection with 'people' is surely incontrovertible? (See *Foclóir Gaedhilge agus Béarla* by Patrick S. Dinneen, Dublin, Irish Texts Society, new edition 1979, and *English-Irish Dictionary* by Tomás de Bhaldraithe, Oifig an tSoláthair, Baile 'Atha Cliath 1959.)

Exclusively synchronic students of language may find some of this hard to swallow, but for the diachronist Quintilius's text is a banquet. As he himself quotes elsewhere from Flavius Vopiscus (Vop. in Bon. 14):

> *ut quantum bibisses, tantum mingeres.*

Finally, further strong corrobberation is to be drawn from the *ta'wîl* (Ismaili esoteric exegesis) on an early Italic fragment of *Cant. Canticorum* (in defective hexameters suspiciously akin to those of Q.) in the Library of the Madrasi-ye Khomeynî at Gorgan, which reads at II. 15:

> *Rapite nobis volpeculas quae populi vineas*
> *Demoliuntur...*

but examination of this revealing text must await the author's forthcoming study 'The Destiny of the Vine in the Islamic Republic of Iran'.

95 'He who follows a line' etc. The reference is no doubt to some kind of a shamanic ritual practised by some of the native tribes who were later exterminated by the white Germanic settlers of Labrador. The sentiment incorporated in the native word *nawāyem*, which Q. rendered in the following line, was plainly subversive and not to be supported by the civilised settlers.

The Fisher-Star and the thread probably relate to some kind of rudimentary astronomical observation by the *indigènes,* a theme Q. reverts to once more in line 118, 'Today is the longest night'. Pytheas had visited Thule (Iceland) in order to measure the longest day on the Arctic Circle. Seven hundred years later Quintilius felt himself more involved with the longest *night*. St Lucy was almost certainly a wolf-emblem for the Roman poet, in spite of his occasional lapses into a sort of sentimental Christianity.

122 'Shadow sticks' is plainly another reference to some kind of primitive astronomical ritual. Some kind of Acadian *reflet Druidique?*

127 'The wolves have taken my butterscotch' may well seem to the modern reader to smack more of André Breton than of the *Bretons anciens* but any such hasty judgment would be quite unjustified. Quintilius, as is well known, even in his most serious and solemn moments of vision and prophecy was subject to sudden and unpredictable *raptus* of sheer buffoonery. The barbarous, and presumably macaronic word which I transcribed (not without some nagging doubts) as *tafoscoti* suggested at first something like 'the darkness of the grave' (there is neither a *phi* nor a *kappa* in the Etruscan alphabet) but somehow I did not feel that Quintilius would at this stage of his apparently quite serious poem revert to anything as commonplace (for him) as the ancient Greek culture. It then struck me that the word might be some sort of a compound indicating possible North British companions on his voyage, a possible exogamic union between Welshmen and Scotti long before the days of the Kingdom of Dalriada, but even that did not satisfy my pernickety and I fear pedantic philological conscience. I had to paw over the solution to this sticky problem for some days before the solution came. I should explain that a family of skunks had been sharing our *izba* in Cultus Lake (they lived under the floor and made a lot of noise at night). They were also in the habit of robbing food from our kitchen when we were out gathering roots and berries (as we generally had to be), and one night I dreamed that one of these delightful little animals, enlarged in the dream into the shape of an enormous *wolf*, came into the kitchen and sneaked off with a very large scotch or block of toffee (see Onions, *Oxford Dictionary of English Etymology*, London, 1966, under 'scotch[2]') which my wife had baked for our babe to cut its teeth on. As I woke, intuition came upon me, and I saw quite plainly that the mysterious word could only mean what we moderns call *butterscotch* (which the OED very perfunctorily dismisses, without even a date for its first use, as 'a variety of *toffee*'. On reference to Onions I found that this was a North British word and was earlier written *tuffy, toughy* and *taffy*). By now I realised that it could have nothing to do with anything as gloomy as graves or darkness, or even Welshmen and Scotch, but that the second element of the compound

was Scandinavian *skot* in the sense of shooting, or the thing shot or *cast*, as in *casting* a spell, or *forging* an object or shooting crap. The doubt remained whether the object was a piece of *taffy* or perhaps a *thread* (or lock of hair perhaps, Old Norse *toppr*, Norwegian *tuppa*). The latter interpretation would of course bring it into line with 'following a line' and so perhaps be more *magical* and ritual in its connotations, but I chose the former explanation on the grounds that (1) it had been divinely revealed to the translator in a dream, (2) since there had been no buffoonery in the poem so far, it was in line with Quintilius's other works and constant practice and it was really *de rigueur* to have a little light-hearted playfulness even in an otherwise entirely serious poem.

And if any reader still doubts the authentically Scandinavian connections of this remarkable *kvaethi* (surely closely connected with the classical *qasîda*?) of the African Quintilius, they have but to look to the penultimate verse. Surely there can be no doubts whatsoever as to the far-reaching influence, even in the Scandinavian world, of this visionary buffoon? Q. was anything but monkish. Even if the tin came from the Cassiterides.

I feel it incumbent on me, however, to add a rider to this perhaps over-detailed commentary. That is, I would suggest that those who wish to enjoy 'the poem itself' (*pace* Mr Burnshaw, and the B.B.C. and Mr Derek Parker) should entirely ignore the commentary so as to have a clearer idea of what the poet really said. The commentaries of scholars and critics are often interesting in themselves but all too rarely, as both Lord Bacon and John Donne remarked in startlingly familiar terms, get to grips with what the poem is really about. The commentary, like this one, may be exemplary, but the poem remains, and this poem is surely a very serious and profound one? As Mme de Stael wrote: 'L'énigme de la destinée humaine n'est de rien pour la plupart des hommes; le poète l'a toujours présenté à l'imagination. L'idée de la mort, qui décourage les esprits vulgaires, rend le génie plus audacieux, et le mélange des beautés de la nature et des terreurs de la destruction excite je ne sais quel délire de bonheur et d'effroi, sans lequel l'on ne peut ni comprendre ni déduire le spectacle de ce monde.' The incredulity that is the faith of our time, fostered by the State and the Academies alike, would do well to ponder this. Instead of pouring out money on the latest Kensington 'Cultus' (*vide supra*) which, once abstracted from the sphere of the stable, attracts attention more from the olfactory faculty than from the intelligence or the imagination, it should look to the products of the creative *mind* and encourage an *esprit de grande envergure*. This I maintain is precisely what Quintilius embarked on some sixteen centuries ago and it is plain that he found his inspiration among the bards and wizards of the archaic peoples rather than in the mental *boutiques* and minimal art bazaars of the metropolis and the provincial *civitates*. In the world of commerce and war he may not have been a very heroic creature, but in his own elected sphere of values, for him the only authentic stable, he might have cried out in the spirit of *Voluspá:*

'How better can man die than facing fearful odds?'

Odds indeed! When Gwyn Thomas's novel *The Love Man* was published in the U.S.A., the title had to be altered to *The Wolf at Dusk* in order to make it intelligible.

INDEX OF TITLES

The Act of Love, 111
Analogy, 62
'Asses en ont sofert la cuivre', 40

Berlin December, 44
Blind Homer, 60
A Bone-Rattle, 94
Boy Riding, 61
Brock, 116

A Celebration, 41
Charisma, 87
Claire de Lune, 52
Colophon, 101

Daunia, 24
The Dead Theatre, 75
Delphi, 60
Dream Song, 64

Elegiac, 53
The Elegies of Quintilius, 24
Elegy at the Winter Solstice, 120
Elementary, 119
Evening in a Moroccan Café, 38

'Fallen Sie Langsam', 59
For Ezra Pound's Eightieth
    Birthday, 70
Four Snowmen and a Fifth, 106
From a Hospital Window, 77

Girl Painting, 68
The Golden Age, 26
The Golden Chain, 67

The Holy Virgin of Mileševa, 96
Homage to Henri Rousseau, 18

In a Suburban Garden, 85
In Memoriam. Osip Emilyevich
    Mandelshtam, 100
In the Campo de la Bragora, 66
Interim, 73

Jajce, 88

Leaving Germany, 63

Manuela's Poems, 90
Melos, 21
Memory, 37
Missing a Bus, 56
Mnemosyne, 78
Monday Morning, 51
Moscow the Third Rome, 82
Mousai, 46

Night Resonance, 71
Nineteen Thirty-Seven, 19
Nineteen Twenty-Three, 81

Ode, 14
Ode, 15
Ode to Evening, 20

Plum-Picking 1939, 83
Poem for Peace, 13
The 'Progresse', 126

The River, 69
The Ruin, 22
The Ruins of Madâ'in, 34

Smoke, 105
Snodgrass Who Died Last Week, 16
Splitting the Century, 79
Surya's Dance, 17

Theorem, 109
Three Songs, 48
Tristia, 33
Tsara, 89

Un país de pajaros, 105

Venice in Winter, 72
Verses Written in the Sand, 65

Weihnachten, 47
Winged Amor Painted Blind, 50